Dies irae
concertato

Recent Researches in Music

A-R Editions publishes seven series of critical editions, spanning the history of Western music, American music, and oral traditions.

Recent Researches in the Music of the Middle Ages and Early Renaissance
   Charles M. Atkinson, general editor

Recent Researches in the Music of the Renaissance
   James Haar, general editor

Recent Researches in the Music of the Baroque Era
   Christoph Wolff, general editor

Recent Researches in the Music of the Classical Era
   Eugene K. Wolf, general editor

Recent Researches in the Music of the Nineteenth and Early Twentieth Centuries
   Rufus Hallmark, general editor

Recent Researches in American Music
   John M. Graziano, general editor

Recent Researches in the Oral Traditions of Music
   Philip V. Bohlman, general editor

Each edition in *Recent Researches* is devoted to works by a single composer or to a single genre. The content is chosen for its high quality and historical importance, and each edition includes a substantial introduction and critical report. The music is engraved according to the highest standards of production using our own proprietary software called MusE.

For information on establishing a standing order to any of our series, or for editorial guidelines on submitting proposals, please contact:

A-R Editions, Inc.
801 Deming Way
Madison, Wisconsin 53717

800 736-0070 (U.S. book orders)
608 836-9000 (phone)
608 831-8200 (fax)
http://www.areditions.com

Recent Researches in the Music of the Nineteenth and Early Twentieth Centuries, 25

Stefano Pavesi

Dies irae concertato

Edited by Rey M. Longyear

A-R Editions, Inc.
Madison

Respectfully dedicated to
Maestro Giuseppe Zanaboni
of Piacenza

A-R Editions, Inc., Madison, Wisconsin 53717
© 1998 by A-R Editions, Inc.

All rights reserved. No part of this book may be reproduced or transmitted in any form by any electronic or mechanical means (including photocopying, recording, or information storage and retrieval) without permission in writing from the publisher.

The purchase of this work does not convey the right to perform it in public, nor to make a recording of it for any purpose. Such permission must be obtained in advance from the publisher.

A-R Editions is pleased to support scholars and performers in their use of *Recent Researches* material for study or performance. Subscribers to any of the *Recent Researches* series, as well as patrons of subscribing institutions, are invited to apply for information about our "Copyright Sharing Policy."

Printed in the United States of America

ISBN 0-89579-401-2
ISSN 0193-5364

♾ The paper used in this publication meets the minimum requirements of the American National Standard for Information Sciences—Permanence of Paper for Printed Library Materials, ANSI Z39.48-1984.

Contents

Acknowledgments vi

Introduction vii
  Pavesi's Life vii
  Italian Church Music of the *Primo Ottocento* vii
  Pavesi's *Dies irae concertato* viii
  Notes ix

Text and Translation x

Plates xii

Dies irae concertato
  1. Dies irae 3
  2. Tuba mirum 36
  3. Quid sum miser 64
  4. Rex tremendae 75
  5. Juste judex 91
  6. Inter oves 115
  7. Confutatis 128
  8. Oro supplex 144
  9. Finale 159

Critical Report 177
  The Sources 177
  Editorial Methods 178
  Critical Notes 178

Appendix: Cadenzas 181

Acknowledgments

For the preparation of this edition, I am indebted to the staffs of the library of the Conservatorio "G. Verdi" in Milan and the Biblioteca Comunale and Municipio in Crema; to the data entry skills of Julia Eastin; and to the advice of Lynette Marcello Ritz (violin) and Lori White (voice), who beautifully performed the "Quid sum miser," along with Kate Covington, organist, for the musical illustration when I presented a paper on this work at the international conference "Patronage, Politics, Art and Music in Italy, 1738–1861" held at the University of Louisville in March 1989. Thanks are also due to the editorial staff of A-R Editions. Grants from the National Endowment for the Humanities and the University of Kentucky Research Foundation facilitated much of the initial investigation. I am most grateful of all for the assistance and support of my wife Katherine.

Introduction

Pavesi's Life

Stefano Pavesi (1779–1850) belonged to the generation of composers that dominated Italian opera at the opening of the nineteenth century but was soon eclipsed by Rossini's meteoric rise. Though Pavesi's church music is virtually unknown today, it represents some of the best Italian concerted church music of the nineteenth century.

Pavesi was born in Casaletto Vaprio and had his first music study in Crema, the city nearest his birthplace. While a student in Naples, Pavesi participated in the revolution of 1799, was denounced and imprisoned after its suppression (allegedly, Cimarosa personally interceded to prevent his execution), and was subsequently deported to France. He became a bandsman (playing the serpent) in Napoleon's army and after the battle of Marengo (1800) remained in Italy. He scored his first operatic success in 1805 with *Fingallo e Comala*, the first Italian opera to an Ossianic text, in Venice; his generally recognized operatic masterpiece was *Ser Marcantonio* of 1810, a comic opera with a plot most successfully used by Donizetti in *Don Pasquale*.

After the Austrian occupation of northern Italy in 1814, Pavesi returned to Crema, where he shared the task of musical director at the cathedral with Giuseppe Gazzaniga (1743–1818) and succeeded him in this position in 1818, the year of the *Dies irae concertato*. Though Pavesi continued to write operas until a stroke after the failure of *Fenella* (1831, to a libretto similar to Auber's earlier *La Muette de Portici*) effectively ended his career, his main creative outlet after 1818 was church music.[1]

Italian Church Music of the *Primo Ottocento*

Foreign visitors to Italy during the first half of the nineteenth century were virtually unanimous in their deprecation of Italian church music. Early in the century Alexandre Choron described the most common style, the "style d'église concerté," as one that often "scarcely differs from the theatrical style," and at times is in "the most familiar theatrical style."[2] Jane Watts in 1817 described the Italian music of Holy Week as "Force is stretched into roar;—softness dwindled into whine."[3] In 1828 Franz Sales Kandler wrote that "softness and sweet insipidity, which had their beginning at the end of the eighteenth century, exercise their pernicious influence even at the present day in all the churches in Italy."[4] Italians were no less harsh; in 1838 Cardinal Ostini complained about a church music that was in a "bizarre, indecent, and profane style . . . scandal up to sacrilege."[5]

Present-day writers have shown less polemical fervor against the Italian church music of this period yet still lack enthusiasm for it. Giorgio Pestelli pointed out the "musical bilingualism of the Mass"—resulting from the activity of such operatic composers as Jommelli, Anfossi, and Galuppi as musical directors of important churches—and the adoption of "the language of *opera seria*" in the Neapolitan Mass.[6] Vincenzo Terenzio aptly described the problems of Pavesi's generation of church music composers, noting that the solo passages showed the influence of operatic styles, whereas the choral passages, unless written by a skilled contrapuntist, tended usually to simple harmonic structures and simple harmonic formulae. Church music became "a synthesis which, however, could hardly stand autonomously and remained superficial."[7] It is hoped that this edition of Pavesi's *Dies irae concertato* (1818), perhaps the most significant piece of Italian church music to be composed between the *Stabat mater* of Boccherini (1781, second version 1800) and that of Rossini (1832, second version 1841), will give today's musicians an opportunity to better judge the validity of blanket dismissals of Italian church music of the *primo ottocento*.

Leopold Kantner set up three categories of composers of Italian church music: opera composers who also wrote church music (Cherubini, Donizetti, Rossini); church music composers who also wrote operas (Zingarelli, Gazzaniga, Basili); and the group to which Pavesi belonged, those who turned to church music after a career of writing operas.[8] The support for church music in nineteenth-century Italy depended strongly on the locale and the presiding bishop. The small Piedmontese city of Novara, for instance, enjoyed in succession the services of Pietro Generali (from 1827 to 1832), Saverio Mercadante (from 1833 to 1840), and Carlo Coccia (from 1840 until his death in 1873 shortly before his ninety-first birthday). The composer Giovanni Pacini described splendid performances in Florence during the early 1840s of masses by such German and Italian composers as Paer, Cherubini, Morlacchi, Joseph and Michael Haydn, Mozart, Beethoven, and Winter.[9] On the other hand, the cardinal archbishop of Milan forbade church orchestras in the archdiocese in 1833,[10] and stringed instruments were banned in churches of Rome in 1842 by order of the Vicar General.[11]

Crema, then and now, was relatively isolated but enjoyed a strong tradition of church music under Gazzaniga and then Pavesi. Particularly strong were orchestral resources.[12] Examination of Pavesi's church music (he wrote some seventy works in that genre) shows extensive orchestral resources and elaborate solos or duets with solo instrumental obbligatos, especially for violin, viola, and clarinet.[13]

Accustomed as we are to the complete mass settings of Mozart and Haydn as representing the epitome of classical-era church music, and those of Cherubini, Beethoven, and Hummel as expressing an emergent musical romanticism, it is with some surprise that we examine the numerous mass portions of so many Italian composers of those years. Zingarelli, the most prolific of these composers, wrote both complete masses and mass fragments. Pavesi did not write any complete mass settings but only settings of individual mass sections. Rossini and Donizetti wrote mass fragments during their student days.

Such a procedure of setting the Ordinary of the Mass had two main practical aspects to commend it. First of all, with the music being performed as part of a worship service rather than at a concert, the settings were interrupted by prayers, Scripture readings, a homily, and organ interludes, rendering less important tonal or even stylistic organization between them. Secondly, these mass fragments permitted a kind of "mix and match" organization of church music depending on the resources available on a given Sunday or feast day. Berlioz's description of the High Mass he heard in Rome in 1831 as "a nameless monster with a passage of Vaccai for a head, limbs articulated from selected scraps of Pacini, and a ballet of Gallenberg bringing up the body and tail"[14] may well have been just such a mixing of mass settings by various composers.

Pavesi's *Dies irae concertato*

Pavesi's *Dies irae concertato* is divided into nine set-numbers. The opening "Dies irae" utilizes a storm topos familiar from operas such as Gluck's *Iphigénie en Tauride*, Mozart's *Idomeneo*, and Cherubini's *Eliza*.[15] The second number, the "Tuba mirum," does not have the grandiose brass displays of most nineteenth-century requiems, but rather has arpeggiated fanfare-like ritornellos, a brass fanfare which serves as a signifier of the "splendid trumpet" rather than a portrayal of it, and the G of the fanfare as a pivot for Schubert-like common-tone modulations.

The "Quid sum miser" serves as an island of classical repose and stability, a legacy of the late Neapolitan *opera seria*. In contrast, the "Rex tremendae" is in an imposing Sanctus topos, with block-chord harmonies, *forte* dynamics, major mode, and a relatively slow tempo to create an imposing atmosphere, more akin to the typical Haydn Sanctus than to the Handelian grandeur of the comparable section in Mozart's *Requiem*. To create a contrast, the "Salva me fons pietatis" is sung by the solo quartet, with a particularly lovely and effective use near the end of the section where they sing unaccompanied. The ensuing "Recordare" is a soprano-tenor duet, a part of the set-number, but in B-flat major rather than the E-flat major of the opening. The somewhat sentimental chromatic inflections in this duet can often be found in the contemporaneous church music of Catholic (e.g., Hummel) and Protestant (e.g., Spohr) composers; such expressive devices were both ecumenical and international.

The following aria, the "Juste judex," is also in B-flat major, and is an elaborate aria for tenor with clarinet obbligato, with a second clarinet frequently doubling the first in thirds. The cabaletta, "Qui Mariam absolvisti," contains many operatic devices of the time, with a crescendo over an *occhiali*[16] bass and coda piled on coda.

In contrast, the "Inter oves," in F major, is an alto solo with a lightly scored accompaniment and a pastoral topos, and the bass solo, "Oro supplex," is a penitential aria with an extensive viola obbligato. The storm topos, key (D minor), and orchestration of the "Dies irae" recurs in the "Lacrimosa" section of this bass aria; the opening key and mood also recur with the viola solo concluding the aria, effectively conveying the message "Grant them rest."

The finale, exclusively devoted to the text "Amen," is in C major, opening with an extensive and highly-developed double fugue. The ensuing allegro resembles in expression the "dona nobis pacem" of the classical-era mass and provides a *lieto fine* to the work. However, in the full score and relevant vocal parts, a three-measure choral "Amen" was penciled in near the close of the "Oro supplex" (mm. 100–102) while in those same parts, the finale was crossed out. This is possible evidence that at least one performance ended without the finale. Was this because the chorus was unable to sing the double fugue or was it an attempt to provide a more "appropriate" (i.e., restrained) conclusion to the work?[17] In any case, performances of Pavesi's *Dies irae concertato* are documented years after its composition. It was performed in 1835 as part of a program of church music by composers from Crema, in 1850 at Pavesi's funeral, and in 1879 for the centenary of his birth.[18] It may be that for the centennial performance, the *Dies irae concertato* was combined with the *Requiem e Chirie* of 1824 to create a partially complete requiem, for interfiled with many of the parts for the former work are parts in a different hand for the latter.

Notes

1. The only biography so far of Pavesi, which has served as the source for all the preceding information about him, is Fausto Sanseverino's *Notizie intorno da vita e le opere del maestro di musica Stefano Pavesi* (Milan, 1851).

2. Alexandre Choron, *Principes de composition des écoles d'Italie*, 3 vols. (Paris, 1808), 3:24. Pavesi was one of the subscribers to this series (see 1:ix).

3. Jane Watts, *Sketches Descriptive of Italy in the Years 1816 and 1817*, 2 vols. (London, 1820), 2:279.

4. Franz Sales Kandler, "On the Actual State of Music in Rome," *Quarterly Musical Magazine and Review*, 10 (1828): 22. The translator indicated that Kandler "had the assistance of Baini [Palestrina's biographer] and Bandelini" in writing the article.

5. From Ostini's *Editto contro l'abuso* of 27 November 1838, cited in Karl Gustav Fellerer, "Kirchenmusikalische Reformbestrebungen um 1800," *Analecta Musicologica* 21 (1982): 400.

6. Giorgio Pestelli, *The Age of Mozart and Beethoven*, trans. Eric Cross (Cambridge: Cambridge University Press, 1984), 98–99.

7. Vincenzo Terenzio, *La musica italiana nell'ottocento*, 2 vols. (Milan: Bramante Editrice, 1976), 2:606.

8. Leopold Kantner, "Stilistische Stromungen in der Italienischen Kirchenmusik 1770–1830," *Analecta Musicologica* 21 (1982): 380–81, in which neither Pavesi nor his music are mentioned. For a fine overview of church music of the time, see also Kantner's "Kirchenmusik und Oratorium seit der Aufklärung," in Carl Dahlhaus, ed., *Die Musik des 18. Jahrhunderts* (Laaber: Laaber-Verlag, 1985), 372–83.

9. Giovanni Pacini, "La musica sacra in Toscana," *Gazzetta musicale di Milano*, 31 July 1842, 137.

10. *Allgemeine musikalische Zeitung* 35 (1833), col. 799.

11. *Gazzetta musicale di Milano*, 23 October 1842, 184.

12. Sanseverino, 28.

13. For a catalogue of Pavesi's church music, see the *Catalogo di tutti i pezzi di musica sacra dell'Esimio Maestro Stefano Pavesi* (undated manuscript, Biblioteca Comunale, Crema).

14. David Cairns, ed. and trans., *The Memoirs of Hector Berlioz* (London: Gollancz, 1969), 185.

15. For specimens of operatic storm topoi, see Gudrun Busch, "Die Unwetterszene in der romantischen Oper," in Heinz Becker, ed., *Die 'Couleur locale' in der Oper des 19. Jahrhunderts* (Regensburg: Gustav Bosse Verlag, 1976), 161–212, with those of the early Italian opera discussed on pp. 186–89.

16. The Italian term for "eyeglasses," in reference to the shorthand notation .

17. I discuss the work in greater detail in my article, "From Classic to Romantic in Italian Church Music: The *Dies Irae Concertato* of Stefano Pavesi," in Marian Green, ed., *Patronage, Politics, Art and Music in Italy, 1738–1861* (forthcoming).

18. For the 1835 and 1879 performances, see Bice Benvenuti, *La Musica in Crema* (Crema, 1881), 29. For the 1850 performance, see *Solenne uffizio di suffragio a Stefano Pavesi maestro di cappella nella cattedrale di Crema* (Crema: privately printed, 1850), 4.

Text and Translation

The *Dies irae* text presented below is based on that of the *Liber Usualis*, except in the case of "seculum" ("Dies irae," line 2) which reads "saeclum" in *LU*. The translation is from *Translations and Annotations of Choral Repertoire, Volume I: Sacred Latin Texts*, compiled and annotated by Ron Jeffers (Corvallis, Ore.: earthsongs, 1988). © 1988 by earthsongs; reprinted by permission.

1. Dies irae

Dies irae, dies illa,
Solvet seculum in favilla:
Teste David cum Sibylla.
Quantus tremor est futurus,
Quando judex est venturus,
Cuncta stricte discussurus!

Day of wrath, that day
shall dissolve the world into embers,
as David prophesied with the Sibyl.
How great the trembling will be,
when the Judge shall come,
the rigorous investigator of all things!

2. Tuba mirum

Tuba mirum spargens sonum
Per sepulcra regionum,
Coget omnes ante thronum.
Mors stupebit et natura,
Cum resurget creatura,
Judicanti responsura.
Liber scriptus proferetur,
In quo totum continetur,
Unde mundus judicetur.
Judex ergo cum sedebit,
Quidquid latet apparebit:
Nil inultum remanebit.

The trumpet, spreading its wondrous sound
through the tombs of every land,
will summon all before the throne.
Death will be stunned, likewise nature,
when all creation shall rise again
to answer the One judging.
A written book will be brought forth,
in which all shall be contained,
and from which the world shall be judged.
When therefore the Judge is seated,
whatever lies hidden shall be revealed,
no wrong shall remain unpunished.

3. Quid sum miser

Quid sum miser tunc dicturus?
Quem patronum rogaturus?
Cum vix justus sit securus.

What then am I, a poor wretch, going to say?
Which protector shall I ask for,
when even the just are scarcely secure?

4. Rex tremendae

Rex tremendae majestatis,
Qui salvandos salvas gratis,
Salva me, fons pietatis.

King of terrifying majesty,
who freely saves the saved:
Save me, fount of pity.

Recordare Jesu pie,
Quod sum causa tuae viae:
Ne me perdas illa die.
Quaerens me, sedisti lassus:
Redemisti crucem passus:
Tantus labor non sit cassus.

5. Juste judex

Juste judex ultionis,
Donum fac remissionis,
Ante diem rationis.
Ingemisco, tamquam reus:
Culpa rubet vultus meus:
Supplicanti parce Deus.
Qui Mariam absolvisti,
Et latronem exaudisti,
Mihi quoque spem dedisti.
Preces meae non sunt dignae:
Sed tu bonus fac benigne,
Ne perenni cremer igne.

6. Inter oves

Inter oves locum praesta,
Et ab haedis me sequestra,
Statuens in parte dextra.

7. Confutatis

Confutatis maledictis,
Flammis acribus addictis,
Voca me cum benedictis.

8. Oro supplex

Oro supplex et acclinis,
Cor contritum quasi cinis:
Gere curam mei finis.
Lacrimosa dies illa,
Qua resurget ex favilla
Judicandus homo reus:
Huic ergo parce Deus.
Pie Jesu Domine,
Dona eis requiem.

9. Finale

Amen.

Remember, merciful Jesus,
that I am the cause of your sojourn;
do not cast me out on that day.
Seeking me, you sat down weary;
having suffered the Cross, you redeemed me.
May such great labor not be in vain.

Just Judge of vengeance,
grant the gift of remission
before the day of reckoning.
I groan, like one who is guilty;
my face blushes with guilt.
Spare thy supplicant, O God.
You who absolved Mary,
and heeded the thief,
have also given hope to me.
My prayers are not worthy,
but Thou, good one, kindly grant
that I not burn in the everlasting fires.

Grant me a favored place among thy sheep,
and separate me from the goats,
placing me at thy right hand.

When the accursed are confounded,
consigned to the fierce flames:
call me to be with the blessed.

I pray, suppliant and kneeling,
my heart contrite as if it were ashes:
protect me in my final hour.
O how tearful that day,
on which the guilty shall rise
from the embers to be judged.
Spare them then, O God.
Merciful Lord Jesus,
grant them rest.

Amen.

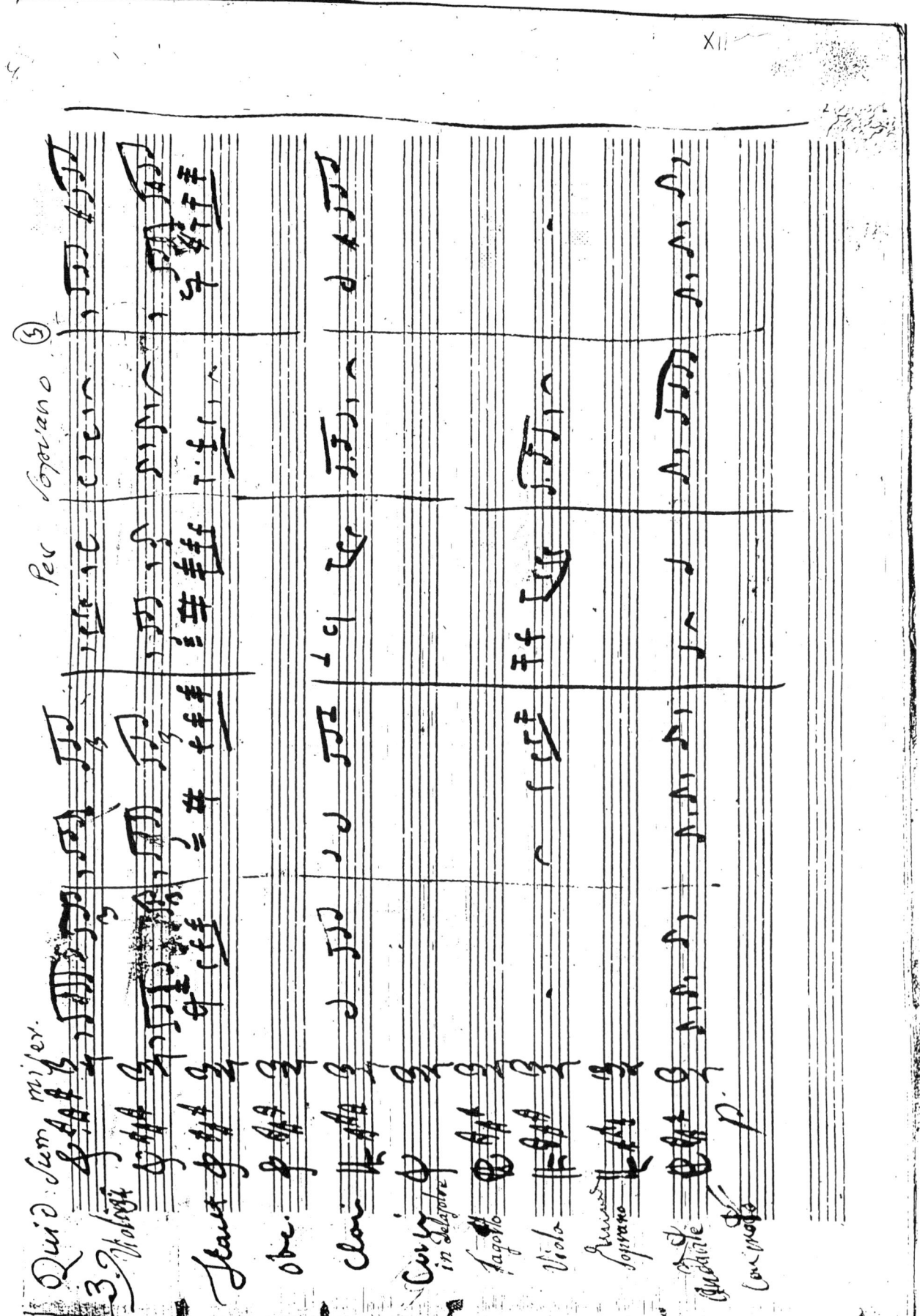

Plate 1. Stefano Pavesi, *Dies irae concertato*, autograph score, first page of "Quid sum miser." Courtesy of the Municipio di Crema and the Biblioteca Comunale di Crema.

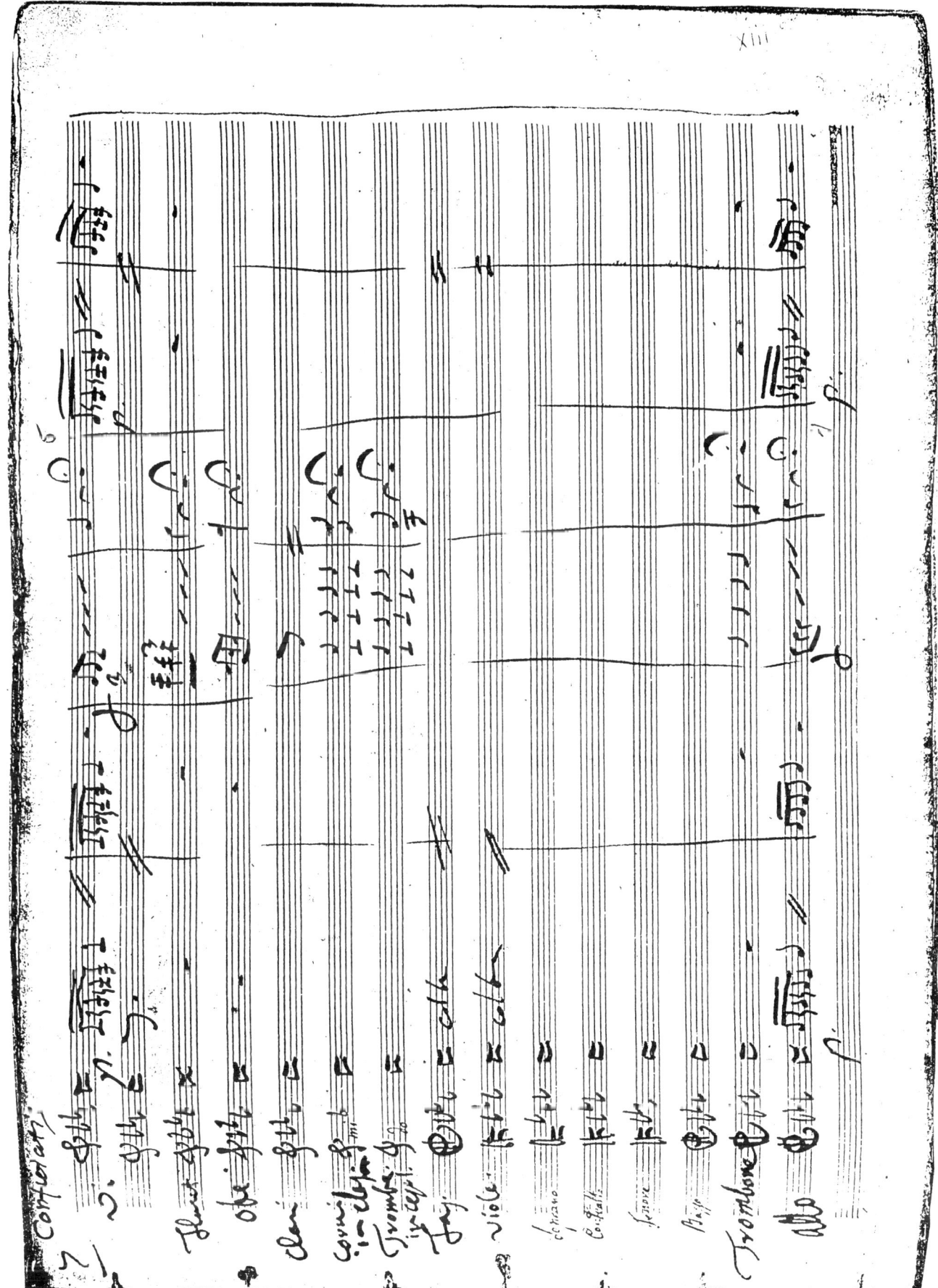

Plate 2. Stefano Pavesi, *Dies irae concertato*, autograph score, first page of "Confutatis." Courtesy of the Municipio ci Crema and the Biblioteca Comunale di Crema.

Dies irae concertato

VOICES

Chorus

Soprano (S)
Alto (A)
Tenor (T)
Bass (B)

Soloists

Soprano (S)
Alto (A)
Tenor (T)
Bass (B)

INSTRUMENTS

Piccolo (Picc.)
Flute (Fl.) (alternates with piccolo in mvt. 1)
Oboe (Ob.) 1, 2
Clarinet (Cl.) 1, 2
Bassoon (Bn.)
Horn (Hn.) 1, 2
Trumpet (Tpt.) 1, 2
Trombone (Trb.)
Timpani (Timp.)
Violin (Vn.) 1
Violin (Vn.) 2
Viola (Va.)
Violoncello (Vc.)
Contrabass (Cb.)

1. Dies irae

8

78
-su- rus, Cunc- ta stric- te dis cus
-su- rus,
-su- rus, Cunc- ta stric- te dis- cus-
Cunc- ta stric- te dis- cus-

-surus, Cunc- ta stric- te dis- cus- su- rus,

Cunc- ta stric- te dis- cus- su- rus,

-rus, Cunc- ta stric- te dis- cus- su- rus,

-surus, Cunc- ta stric- te dis- cus- su- rus,

dis- cus- su- rus!
dis- cus- su- rus!
dis- cus- su- rus!
dis- cus- su- rus!

24

25

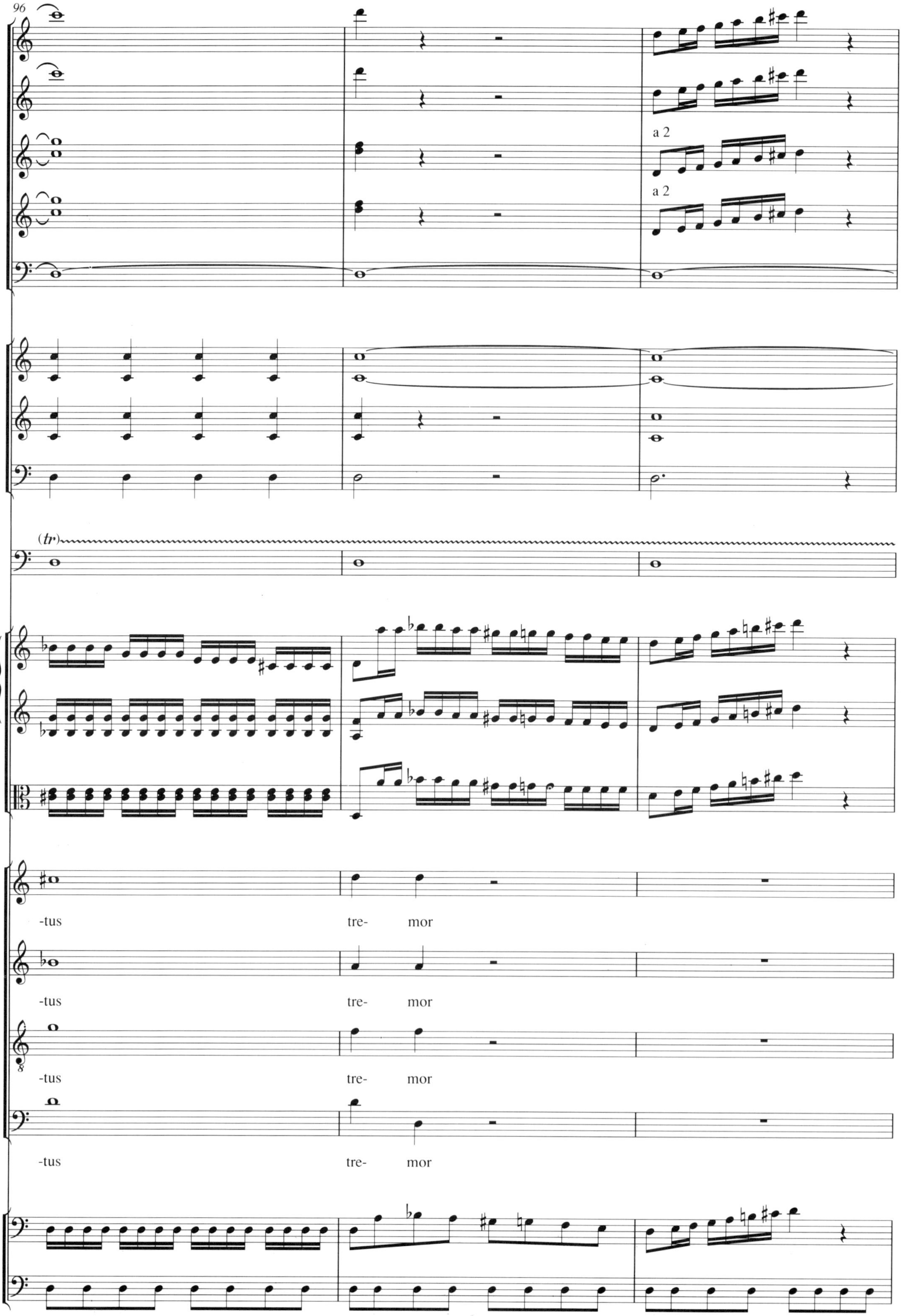
96
a 2
a 2
(tr)
-tus tre- mor
-tus tre- mor
-tus tre- mor
-tus tre- mor

27

fu- tu- rus, Quan- do ju- dex est ven-
fu- tu- rus, Quan- do ju- dex est ven-
fu- tu- rus, Quan- do ju- dex est ven-
fu- tu- rus, Quan- do ju- dex est ven-

-tu- rus, Cunc- ta stric- te dis- cus- su-

-tu- rus, Cunc- ta stric- te dis- cus- su-

-tu- rus, Cunc- ta stric- te dis- cus- su-

-tu- rus, Cunc- ta stric- te dis- cus- su-

30

111
-tu- rus, Cunc ta stric- te dis- cus- su-
-tu- rus, Cunc ta stric- te dis- cus- su-
-tu- rus, Cunc- ta stric- te dis- cus- su-
-tu- rus, Cunc- ta stric- te dis- cus- su-

32

33

34

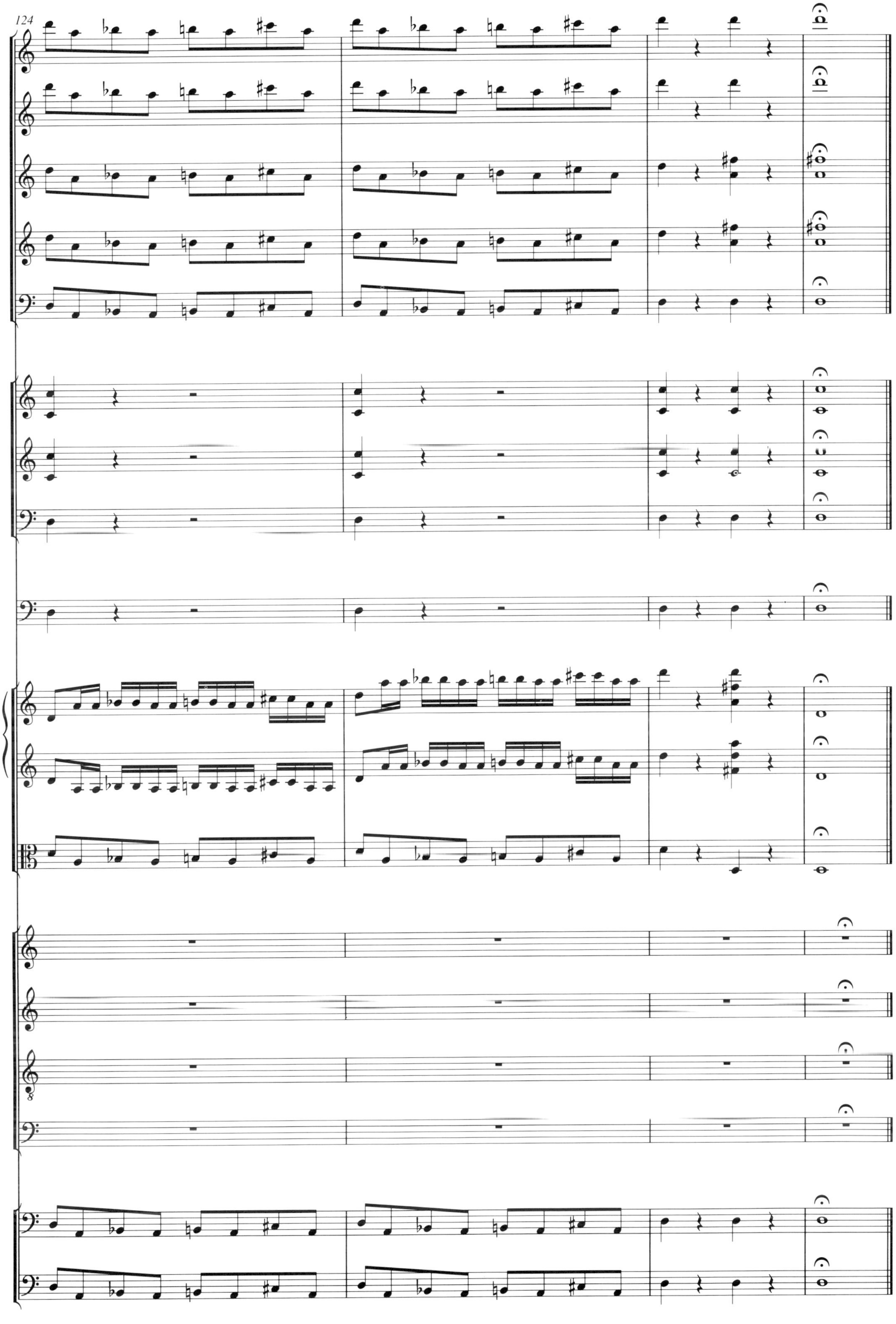
124

2. Tuba mirum

5
p
3
3
3
3
p
p
p
p
p
tutti
ff
Tu- ba mi- rum spar- gens
tutti
ff
ossia
8va
Tu- ba mi- rum spar- gens
tutti
ff
Tu- ba mi- rum spar- gens
tutti
ff
Tu- ba mi- rum spar- gens
p

so- num — Per se- pul- cra re- gi-

39

thro- num, an- te thro- num, an- te thro- num, an- te thro- num, an- te thro- num.

thro num.

thro- num.

thro- num.

il medesimo tempo allegro
28
in E♭
a 2
in B♭
a 2
il medesimo tempo allegro

43

36
-pe- bit et na- tu- ra,
-pe- bit et na- tu- ra,
Cum re- sur- get
-pe- bit et na- tu- ra,

45

46

49
a 2
tutti
-can- ti res- pon- su- ra, Ju- di-
-can- ti res- pon- su- ra, Ju- di-
-can- ti res- pon- su- ra, Ju- di-
-can- ti res- pon- su- ra, Ju- di-

48

-can- ti res- pon- su- ra.

-can- ti res- pon- su- ra.

-can- ti res- pon- su- ra.

-can- ti res- pon- su- ra.

49

In quo totum continetur, Unde mundus,

mun- dus ju- di- ce- tur.

mun- dus ju- di- ce- tur.

[tutti] *f*
Un- de mun- dus ju- di- ce- tur.

mun- dus ju- di- ce- tur.

73
soli
p
soli
p
p
p
p
p
p
p
ossia
8va
Ju- dex er- go cum se-
Ju- dex er- go cum se-
Ju- dex er- go cum se-
Ju- dex er- go cum se-
p

53

54

Nil in- ul- tum re- ma- ne- bit, Nil in-
-ne- bit Nil in- ul- tum, nil in-
-ne- bit, Nil in- ul- tum, nil in-
-ne- bit, Nil in- ul- tum, nil in-

56

99
a 2
a 2
cum se- de- bit, Quid-
cum se- de- bit, Quid-
cum se- de- bit, Quid-
cum se- de- bit, Quid-

58

Nil in- ul- tum re- ma- ne- bit, Nil in-
Nil in- ul- tum re- ma- ne- bit,
Nil in- ul- tum re- ma- ne- bit,
Nil in- ul- tum re- ma- ne- bit,

116
a 2
a 2
a 2
-ul- tum re- ma- ne- bit, Nil in- ul- tum re- ma-
re- ma- ne- bit, Nil in- ul- tum re- ma-
Nil in- ul- tum re- ma- ne- bit, Nil in- ul- tum re- ma-
Nil in- ul- tum re- ma- ne- bit, Nil in- ul- tum re- ma-

-[ne]- - bit, re- ma- ne-

-bit, re- ma- ne- bit,

re- ma- ne- bit.

3. Quid sum miser

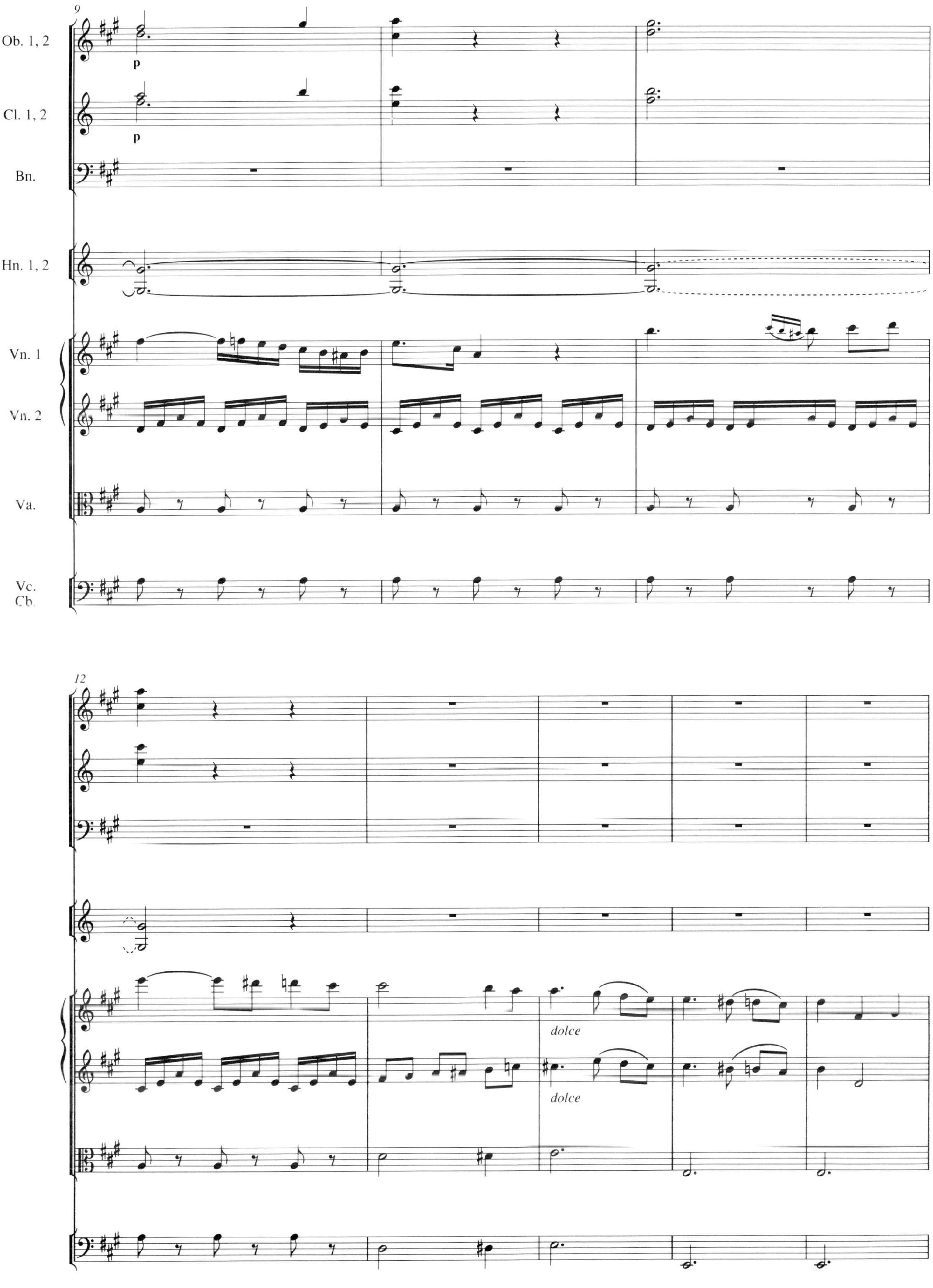
9
Ob. 1, 2
p
Cl. 1, 2
p
Bn.
Hn. 1, 2
Vn. 1
Vn. 2
Va.
Vc.
Cb.
12
dolce
dolce

17
Bn.
Vn. 1
Vn. 2
Va.
S
Quid sum mi- ser, sum mi- ser tunc dic- tu- rus? Quem pa-
Vc.
Cb.
22
Ob. 1, 2
Cl. 1, 2
Bn.
Hn. 1, 2
Vn. 1
Vn. 2
Va.
S
-tro- num ro- ga- tu- rus? Quid sum
Vc.
Cb.

26
a 2
mi- ser tunc dic- tu- rus, Quid sum mi- ser tunc dic- tu- rus?
31
Quem pa- tro- num ro- ga- tu- rus?

68

69

61
Bn.
Vn. 1
Vn. 2
Va.
S
Quid sum mi- ser, sum mi- ser tunc dic- tu- rus? Quem pa- tro- num ro- ga-
Vc.
Cb.
67
Fl.
Ob. 1, 2
Cl. 1, 2
Bn.
Hn. 1, 2
p
Vn. 1
Vn. 2
Va.
S
-tu- rus? Quid sum mi- ser tunc dic-
Vc.
Cb.

72
Bn.
Hn. 1, 2
Vn. 1
Vn. 2
Va.
S
-tu- rus, Quid sum mi- ser tunc dic- tu- rus, tunc dic-
Vc.
Cb.
78
Fl.
Ob. 1, 2
Cl. 1, 2
Bn.
Hn. 1, 2
Vn. 1
Vn. 2
Va.
Cadenza 2
S
-tu- rus? Cum vix jus- tus
Vc.
Cb.

84
p
sit se- cu- rus, sit se- cu- rus,
89
Bn.
Vn. 1
Vn. 2
Va.
S
Cum vix jus- tus sit se- cu- rus, Cum vix
Vc.
Cb.

jus- tus sit se- cu- rus, sit se- cu- rus,

sit _____ se- cu- rus, sit se- cu-

104
Fl.
Ob. 1, 2
Cl. 1, 2
Bn.
Hn. 1, 2
Vn. 1
Vn. 2
Va.
S
Vc.
Cb.
f
p dolce
p
Cadenza 3
-rus, sit se- cu- rus.
108
a 2

4. Rex tremendae

[soli]
soli
solo
gra- tis, Sal- va me, fons pi- e- ta- tis.
solo
gra- tis, Sal- va me, fons pi- e- ta- tis.
solo
gra- tis, Sal- va me, fons pi- e-
solo
gra- tis, Sal- va me, fons pi- e-

a 2
tutti
ff
Rex tre- men- dae ma- jes- ta- tis, Qui sal-
Rex tre- men- dae ma- jes- ta- tis, Qui sal-
-ta- tis. Rex tre- men- dae ma- jes- ta- tis, Qui sal-
-ta- tis. Rex tre- men- dae ma- jes- ta- tis, Qui sal-

78

15
tr
tutti
solo
-ta- tis, fons pie- ta- tis, Sal- va me, fons pi- e- ta- -
tutti
solo
-ta- tis, fons pie- ta- tis, Sal- va me, fons pi- e- ta- -
tutti
solo
-ta- tis, fons pie- ta- tis, fons pi- e- ta-
solo
fons pie- ta- tis, fons pi- e- ta-
Cb.
[tutti]

20
- tis, Sal- va me, fons pie- ta- - tis.
- tis, Sal- va me, fons pie- ta- - tis.
- tis, Sal- va me, fons pie- ta- - tis.
- tis, Sal- va me, fons pie- ta- - tis.

Allegretto
Bn.
p
Allegretto
Vn. 1
Vn. 2
Va.
T
solo
Re- cor- da- re Je- su
pizz.
Vc.
Cb.
Vn. 1
Vn. 2
Va.
S
solo
Re- cor- da- re
T
pi c, Quod sum ca- u- sa tu- ae vi- ae, Re- cor- da- re
Vc.
Cb.

39
Je- su pi- e, Quod sum cau- sa tu- ae vi- ae:
Je- su pi- e, Quod sum cau- sa tu- ae vi- ae:
45
Ob.1, 2
p
a 2
Cl. 1, 2
p
a 2
Hn. 1, 2
a 2
p
Vn. 1
Vn. 2
Va.
S
Ne me per- das il- la di- e. Quae- rens me, se-
T
Ne me per- das il- la di- e.
Vc.
Cb.

51
a 2
p
[divisi]
-di- sti las- sus, se- di- sti las- sus: Re- de- mi- sti
Quae-rens me, se- di- sti las- sus: Re- de- mi- sti cru- cem,
58
Cl. 1, 2
Hn. 1, 2
Vn. 1
Vn. 2
Va.
S
cru- cem pas- sus: Tan- tus la- bor, la- bor non sit cas- sus,
T
cru- cem pas- sus: Tan- tus la- bor non sit cas- sus,
Vc.
Cb.

84

81
Fl.
Ob.1, 2
Cl. 1, 2
Hn. 1, 2
Vn. 1
Vn. 2
Va.
S
T
Vc.
Cb.
soli
p
il- la di- e. Quae- rens me, se- di- sti las-sus: Re- de-
Quae- rens me, se- di- sti las- sus, se- di- sti las-sus: Re- de-
88
-mi- sti cru- cem pas-sus: Tan- tus la- bor non sit
-mi- sti cru- cem pas-sus: Tan- tus la- bor non sit

94
Fl.
Ob.1, 2
Cl. 1, 2
Bn.
Hn. 1, 2
Tpt. 1, 2
Trb.
Vn. 1
Vn. 2
Va.
S
cas- sus, Tan- tus la- bor non sit cas- sus, Re- de-
T
cas- sus, Tan- tus la- bor non sit cas- sus, Re- de-
Vc.
Cb.
arco

-mi- sti cru- cem pas- sus: Tan- tus la- bor non sit

88

112
a 2
a 2
-mi- sti cru- cem pas- sus, Re- de- mi- sti cru- cem
-mi- sti cru- cem pas- sus, Re- de- mi- sti cru- cem

pas- sus.

pas- sus.

5. Juste judex

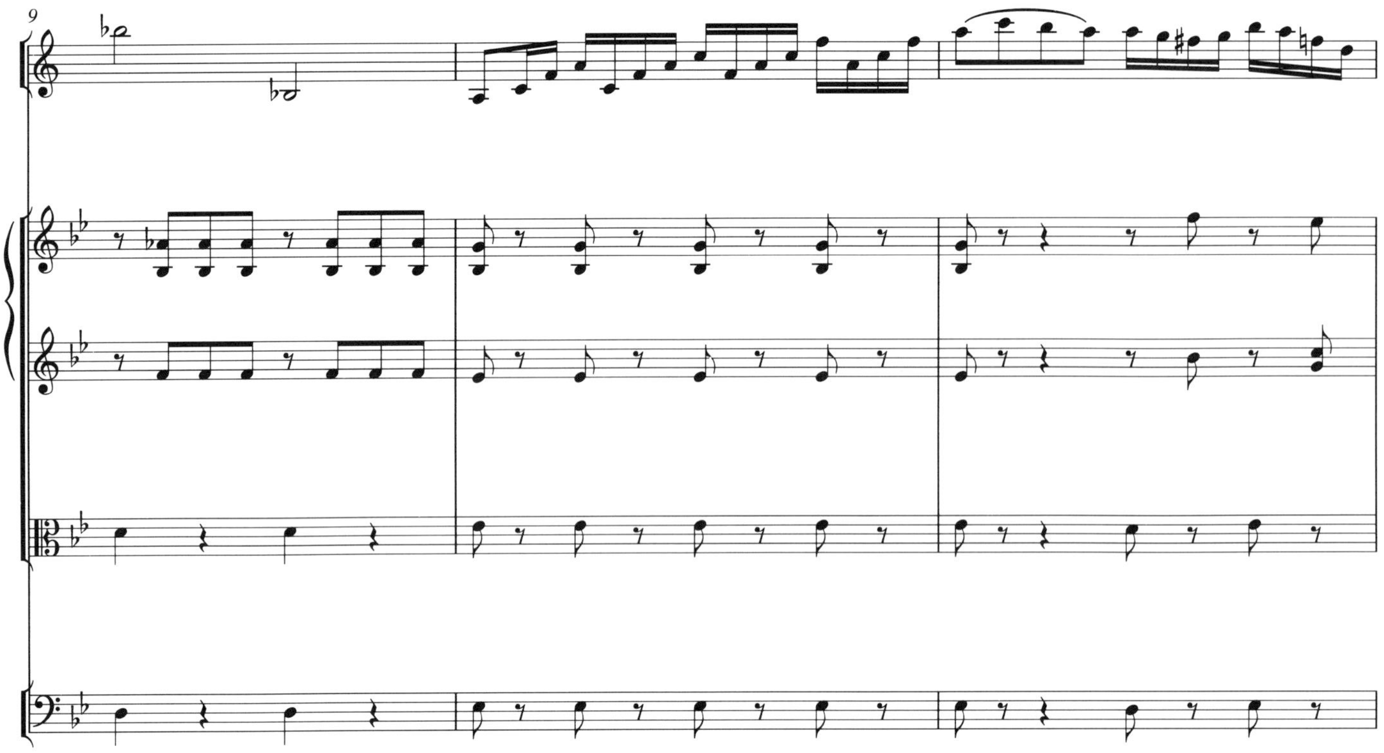
9

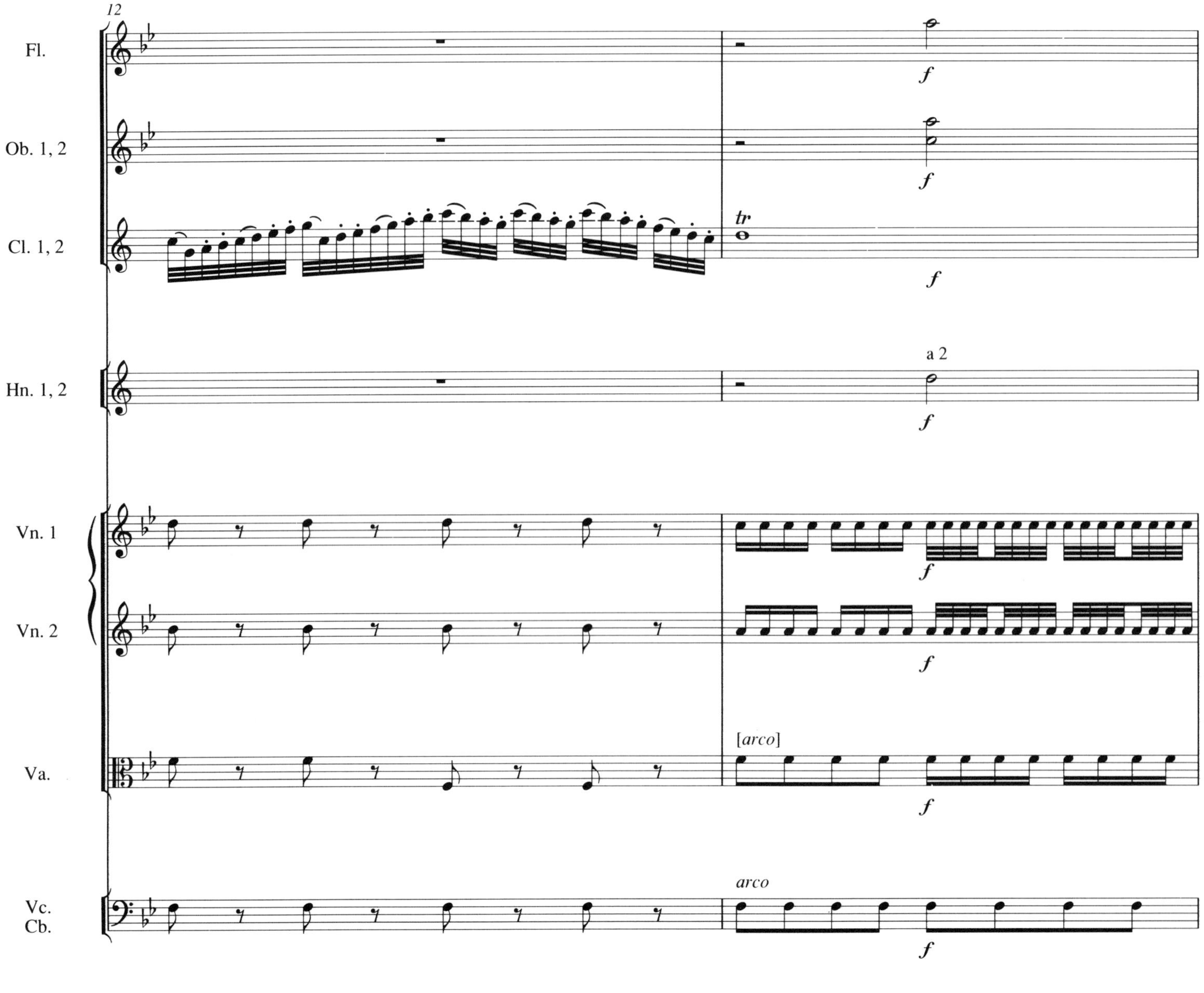
12
Fl.
Ob. 1, 2
Cl. 1, 2
Hn. 1, 2
Vn. 1
Vn. 2
Va.
Vc.
Cb.
tr
a 2
[arco]
arco
f

14
Fl.
Ob. 1, 2
Cl. 1, 2
Bn.
Hn. 1, 2
Tpt. 1, 2
Trb.
Vn. 1
Vn. 2
Va.
T
Jus- te
Vc. Cb.
18
Vn. 1
Vn. 2
Va.
T
ju- dex ul- ti- o- nis, Do- num fac re- mis- si- o- nis, An- te
pizz.
Vc. Cb.

22
soli
mf
Cl. 1, 2
Vn. 1
Vn. 2
Va.
T
di- em ra- ti- o- nis, Do- num
Vc.
Cb.
26
fac re- mis- si- o- nis, An- te di- em ra- ti- o-
30
Fl.
p
Ob. 1, 2
Hn. 1, 2
-nis. In- ge-mis- co, tam-quam re- us:

Cul- pa ru- bet vul- tus me- us, In- ge- mis- co, tam- quam re- us: Cul- pa ru- bet vul- tus me- us: Sup- pli- can- ti par- ce

44
Ob. 1, 2
Cl. 1, 2
solo
mf
Vn. 1
Vn. 2
Va.
T
De- us, par- ce De- - - us.
Vc.
Cb.
48
Bn.
p
In- ge-mis- co, tam- quam re- us: Cul- pa ru- bet vul- tus me- us:
53
Sup- pli- can- ti par- ce De- us, Sup- pli-
arco

-can- ti par- ce De- us.

Allegro
64
Fl.
Ob. 1, 2
Cl. 1, 2
Bn.
Hn. 1, 2
a 2
Tpt. 1, 2
a 2
Trb.
Allegro
Vn. 1
Vn. 2
Va.
T
Vc.
Cb.

Qui Ma- ri- am ab- sol- vi- sti, Et la- tro- nem ex- au-

-di- sti,

Mi- hi quo- que spem de- di- sti, Mi- hi quo- que spem de-

78
Fl.
Ob. 1, 2
Cl. 1, 2
Hn. 1, 2
Vn. 1
Vn. 2
Va.
T
Vc.
Cb.
p
p
soli
mf
a 2
p
a 2
-di- sti. Pre- ces me- ae non sunt
82
solo
dig- nae: Sed tu bo- nus fac be-

-nig- ne, Ne pe- ren- ni cre- mer ig- ne.

96
Fl.
Cl. 1, 2
Hn. 1, 2
Vn. 1
Vn. 2
Va.
T
In- ge- mis- co,
Vc.
Cb.
100
Fl.
Ob. 1, 2
Cl. 1, 2
Hn. 1, 2
Vn. 1
Vn. 2
Va.
T
tam- quam re- us: Cul- pa ru- bet
Vc.
Cb.

104
Fl.
Cl. 1, 2
solo
mf
Hn. 1, 2
Vn. 1
Vn. 2
Va.
T
vul- tus me- us: Sup- pli- can- ti
Vc.
Cb.
108
Cl. 1, 2
Hn. 1, 2
Vn. 1
Vn. 2
Va.
T
par- ce De- us, Sup- pli- can- ti par- ce
Vc.
Cb.

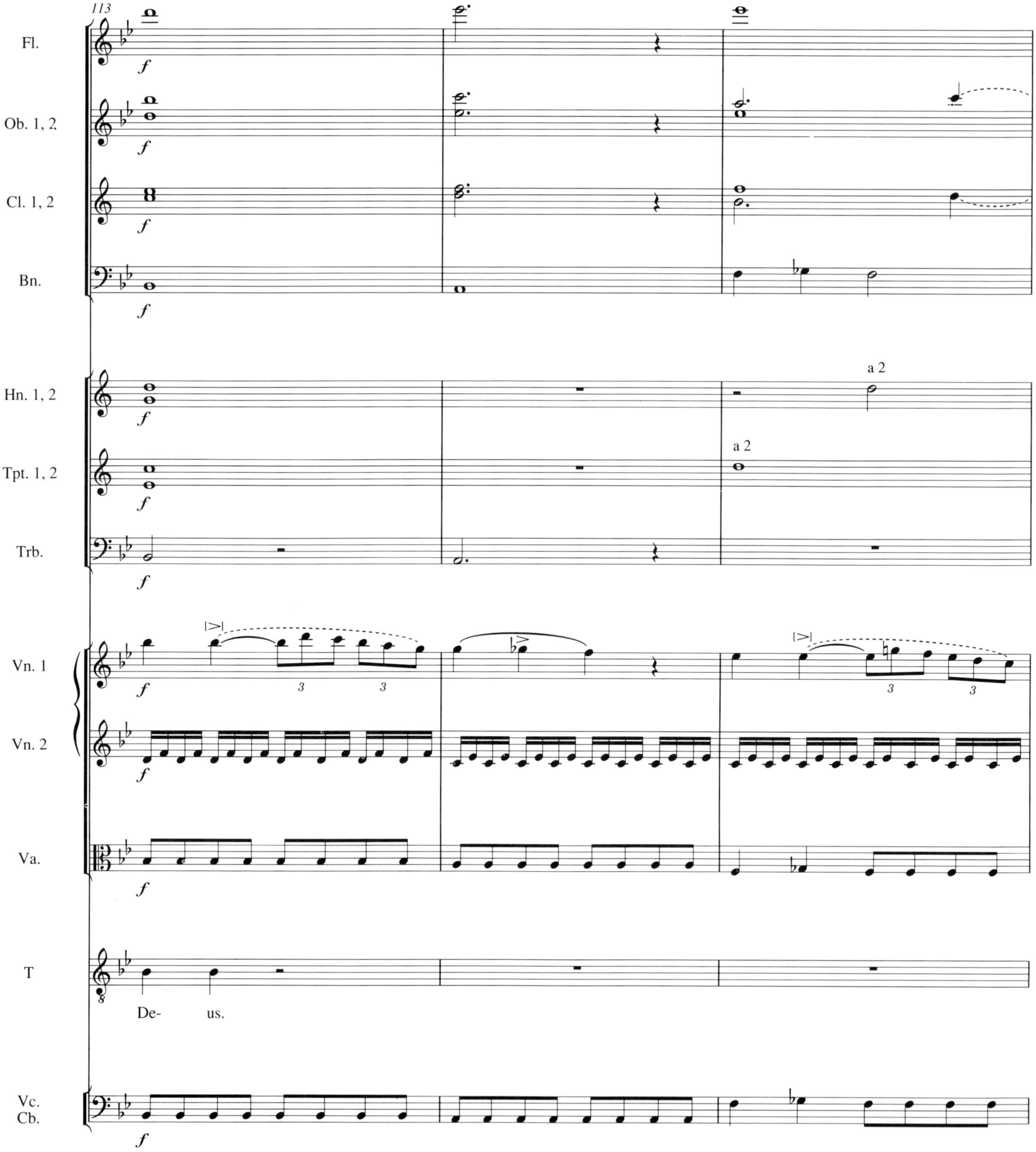
113
Fl.
Ob. 1, 2
Cl. 1, 2
Bn.
Hn. 1, 2
Tpt. 1, 2
Trb.
Vn. 1
Vn. 2
Va.
T
De- us.
Vc.
Cb.
a 2
a 2

Qui Ma- ri- am ab- sol- vi- sti, Et la- tro- nem ex- au- di- sti,

Mi-hi quo- que spem de-

125
Vn. 1
Vn. 2
Va.
T
-di- sti, Mi- hi quo- que spem de- di- sti. Sed tu
Vc. Cb.
129
Fl.
Ob. 1, 2
Cl. 1, 2
Hn. 1, 2
a 2
Vn. 1
Vn. 2
Va.
T
bo- nus fac be- nig- ne, fac be-
Vc. Cb.

133
a 2
a 2
soli
mf
a 2
-nig- ne, Ne pe- ren- ni cre- mer
137
ig- ne, Ne pe- ren- ni cre- mer ig- ne,

142
p
a 2
p
a 2
p
a 2
p
Sed tu bo- nus fac be- nig- ne,
146
[soli]
mf
fac be- nig- ne, Ne pe- ren- ni

150
cre- mer ig- ne, Ne pe- ren- ni cre- mer ig-
155
Fl.
Ob. 1, 2
Cl. 1, 2
Bn.
Hn. 1, 2
Tpt. 1, 2
Trb.
Vn. 1
Vn. 2
Va.
T
Vc.
Cb.
a 2
-ne, Ne pe- ren- ni cre- mer ig- ne, Ne pe-

-ren- ni cre- mer ig- ne,

cre- mer ig- ne.

6. Inter oves

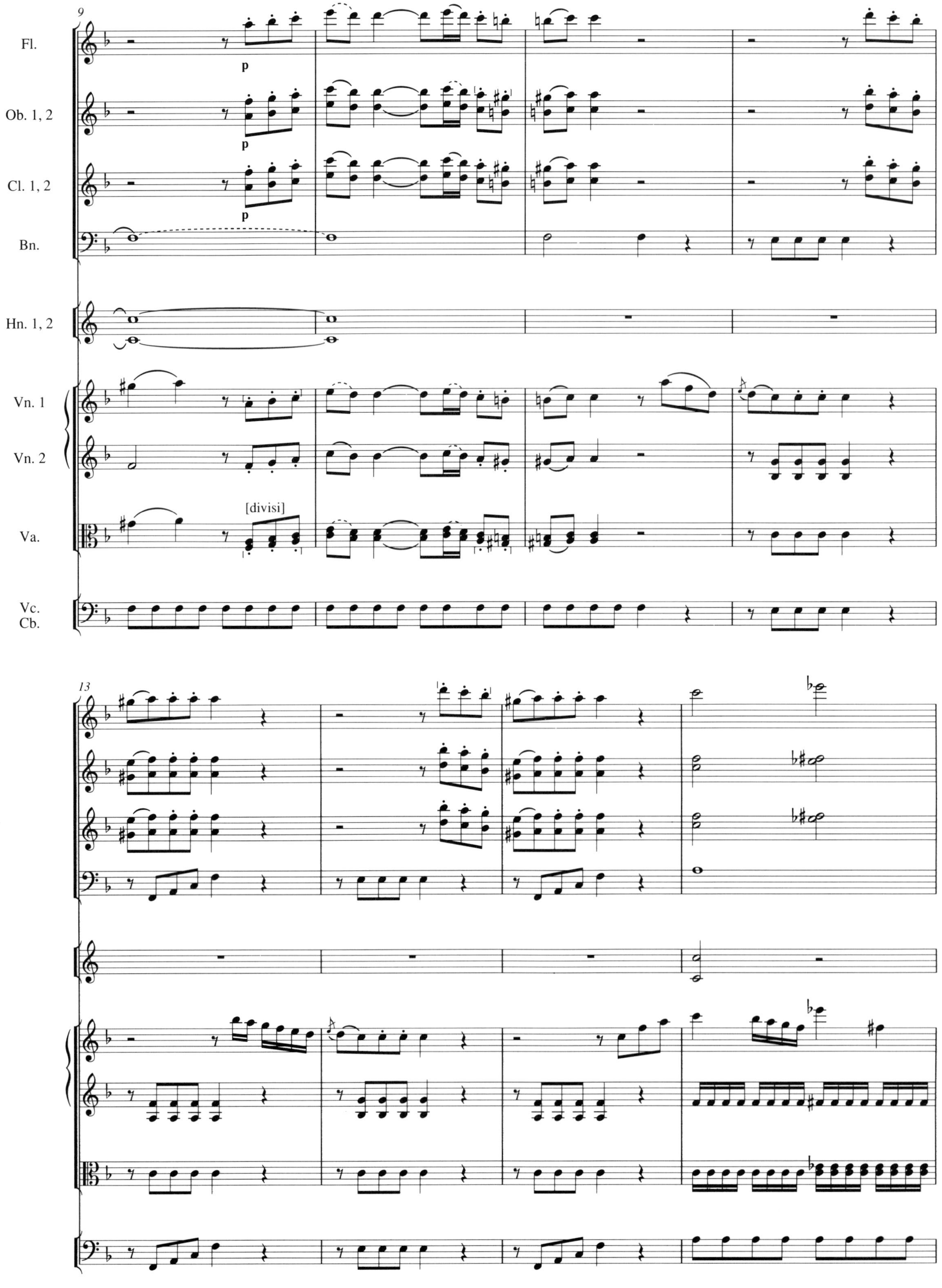
9
Fl.
Ob. 1, 2
Cl. 1, 2
Bn.
Hn. 1, 2
Vn. 1
Vn. 2
Va.
Vc.
Cb.
p
p
p
[divisi]
13

117

24
Vn. 1
Vn. 2
Va.
A
o- ves lo- cum prae- sta, In- ter o- ves lo- cum
Vc.
Cb.
28
Fl.
Ob. 1, 2
Cl. 1, 2
Bn.
Hn. 1, 2
Vn. 1
Vn. 2
Va.
A
prae- sta, Et ab hae- dis me se- ques- tra,
arco
Vc.
Cb.

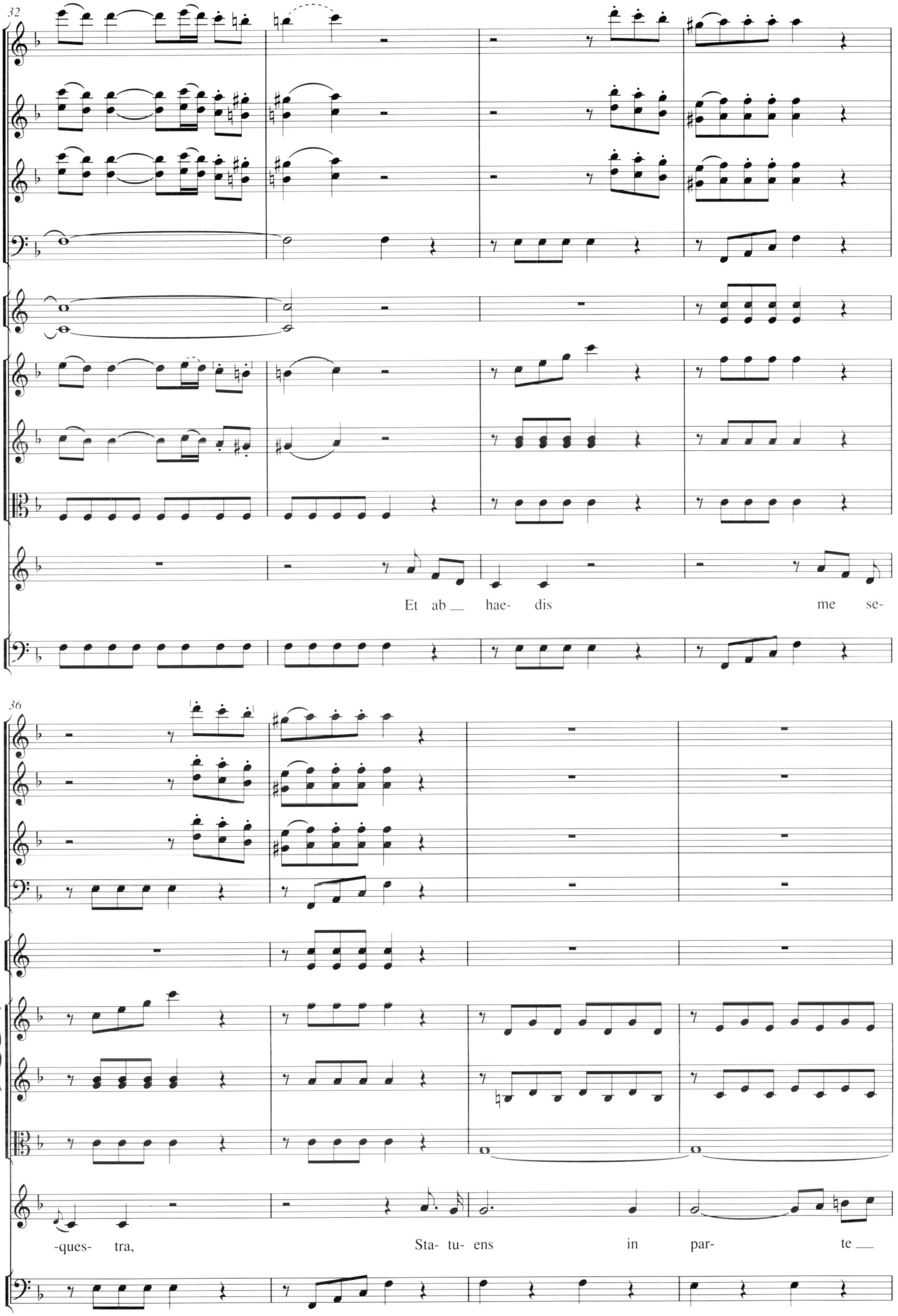
32
Et ab hae- dis me se-
36
-ques- tra,
Sta- tu- ens in par- te

40
a 2
[ossia 8va]
dex- tra, in par- te dex- tra.
44
[soli]
Cl. 1, 2
Vn. 1
Vn. 2
Va.
A
In- ter o- ves lo- cum prae- sta,
Vc.
Cb.

Et ab haedis me sequestra, me sequestra, Statuens in parte dextera,

56
Fl.
Ob. 1, 2
Cl. 1, 2
a 2
Hn. 1, 2
a 2
Vn. 1
Vn. 2
Va.
A
Sta- tu- ens in par- te dex- te- ra.
Vc.
Cb.
60
Vn. 1
Vn. 2
Va.
A
In- ter o- ves lo- cum prae- sta, In- ter
pizz.
Vc.
Cb.

64
Bn.
Hn. 1, 2
Vn. 1
Vn. 2
Va.
A
o- ves lo- cum prae- sta, Et ab haedis me se-
[arco]
Vc.
Cb.
68
Fl.
Ob. 1, 2
Cl. 1, 2
Bn.
Hn. 1, 2
Vn. 1
Vn. 2
Va.
A
-ques- tra, Et ab hae- dis
Vc.
Cb.

124

80
p
dex- te- ra. In- ter o- ves lo- cum
84
Fl.
Cl. 1, 2
Bn.
Hn. 1, 2
Vn. 1
Vn. 2
Va.
A
prae- sta, Et ab hae- dis me se- ques- tra, me se-
Vc.
Cb.

88
Fl.
Ob. 1, 2
Cl. 1, 2
Bn.
a 2
Hn. 1, 2
Vn. 1
Vn. 2
Va.
[ossia]
A
-ques- - - tra, Et ab
Vc.
Cb.
92
tr
hae- dis me se- ques- - -

-tra, me se- ques-

-tra.

7. Confutatis

129

130

131

16
a 2
a 2
a 2
-dic- tis, Con- fu- ta- tis
-dic- tis, Con- fu- ta- tis
-dic- tis, Con- fu- ta- tis
-dic- tis, Con- fu- ta- tis

133

a- cri- bus ad- dic- tis,

28
Fl.
Ob. 1, 2
Cl. 1, 2
Hn. 1, 2
a 2
Vn. 1
Vn. 2
Va.
S
A
T
B
sotto voce
Vo- ca me cum be- ne- dic- tis, cum
Vc.
Cb.
pizz.

be- ne- dic- tis, cum be- ne-
be- ne- dic- tis, cum be- ne-
be- ne- dic- tis, cum be- ne-
be- ne- dic- tis, cum be- ne-

137

42
a 2
tr
-ta- tis ma- le- dic- tis,
-ta- tis ma- le- dic- tis,
-ta- tis ma- le- dic- tis,
-ta- tis ma- le- dic- tis,

139

140

51
Maggiore
Fl.
p
Ob. 1, 2
p
Cl. 1, 2
p
in C
Hn. 1, 2
p
Maggiore
Vn. 1
p
Vn. 2
p
Va.
p
sotto voce
S
Vo- ca me cum be- ne- dic- tis,
sotto voce
A
Vo- ca me cum be- ne- dic- tis,
sotto voce
T
Vo- ca me cum be- ne- dic- tis,
sotto voce
B
Vo- ca me cum be- ne- dic- tis,
pizz.
Vc.
Cb.
p

cum be- ne- dic- tis,

143

8. Oro supplex

145

146

147

et ac- cli- nis, Cor con- tri- tum qua- si

ci- nis,

Cor con-

149

150

66
Allegro
Picc.
Fl.
Ob. 1, 2
Cl. 1, 2
Bn.
Hn. 1, 2
Tpt. 1, 2
Trb.
Timp.
Vn. 1
Vn. 2
Va.
B
Vc.
Cb.
a 2
a 2
in D
in D
tr
Allegro
[tutti]

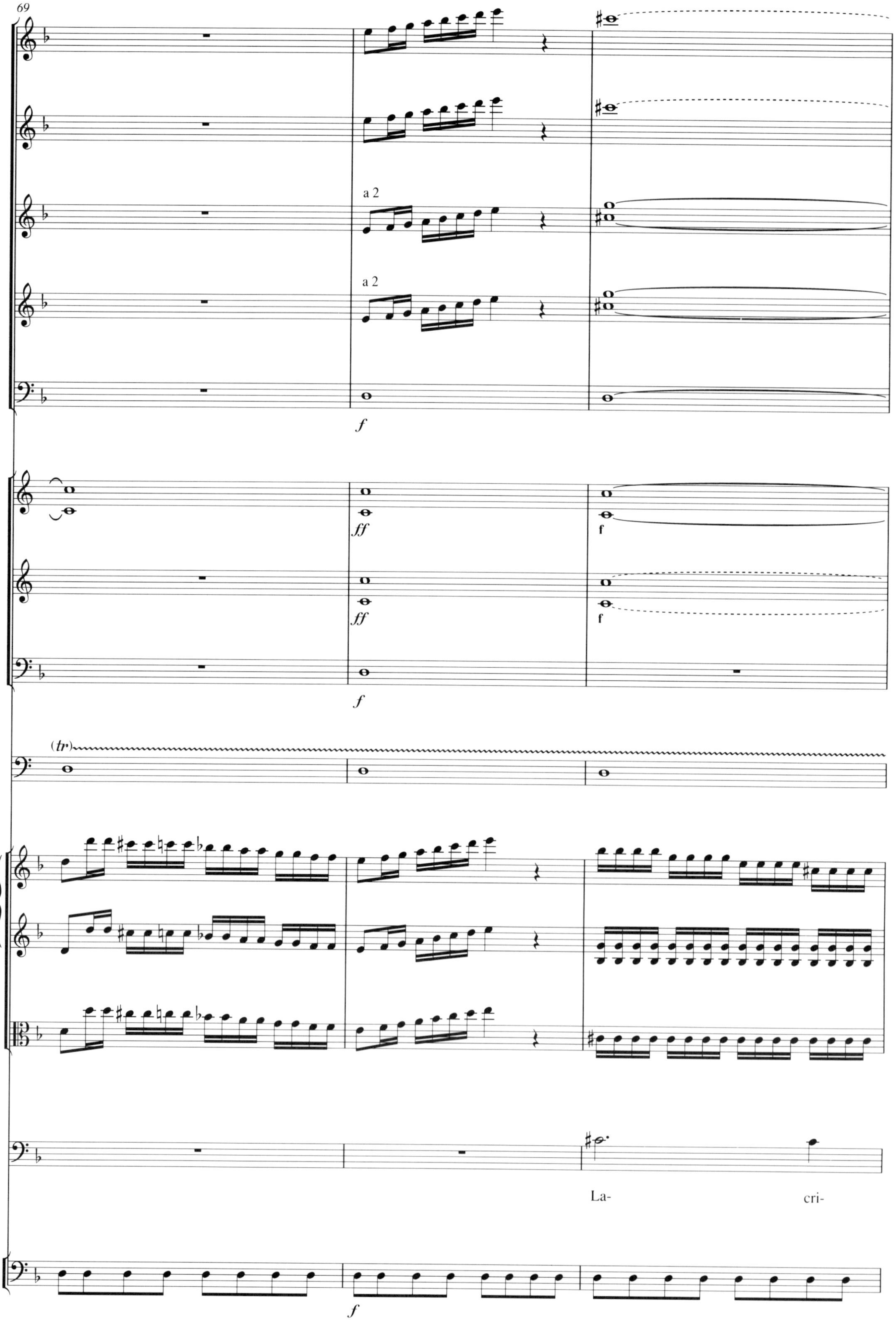
69
a 2
a 2
f
ff
f
ff
f
f
(tr)
La-
cri-
f

-mo- sa di- es il- la,

154

-sur- get ex fa- vil- la Ju- di-

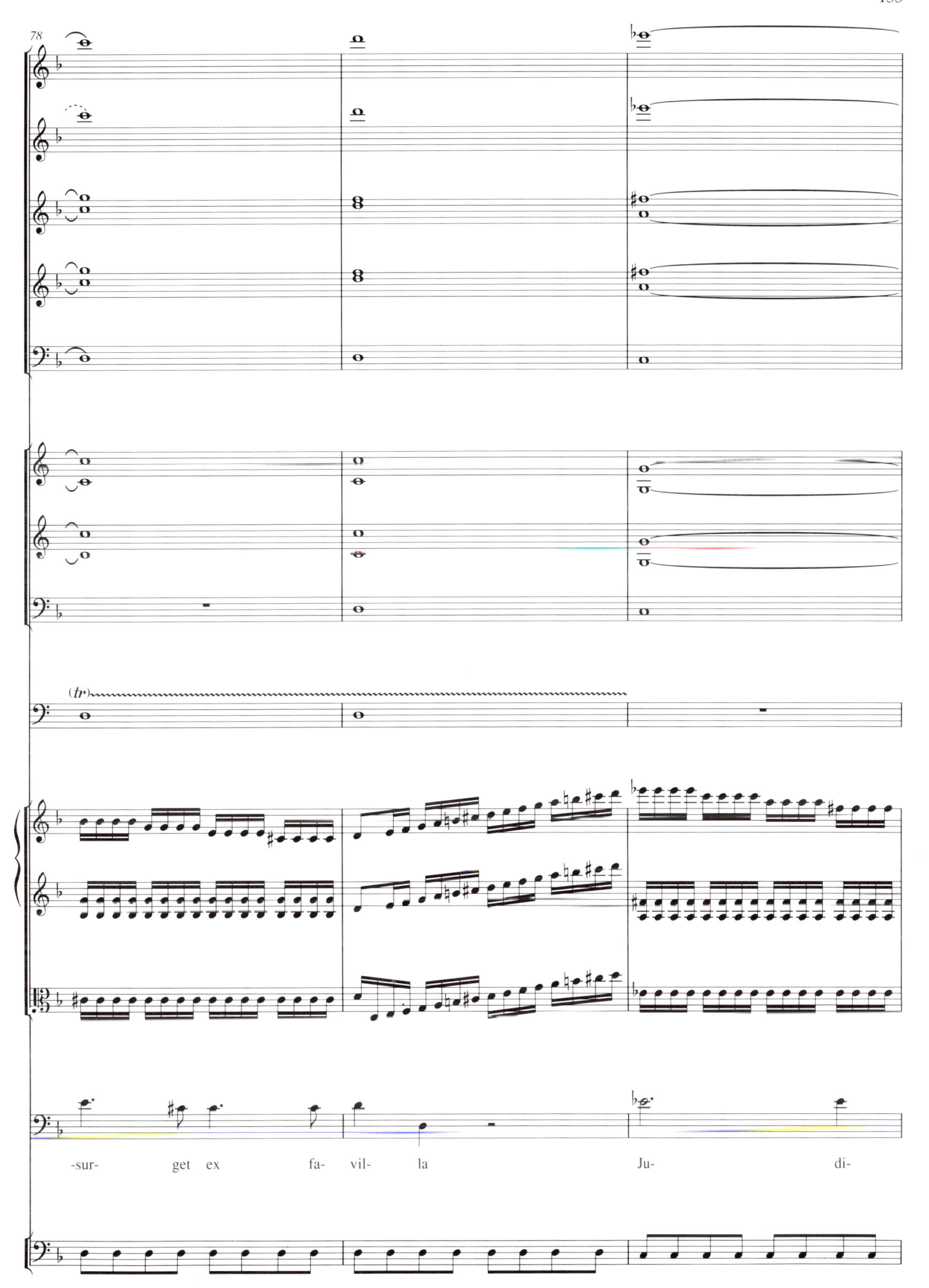

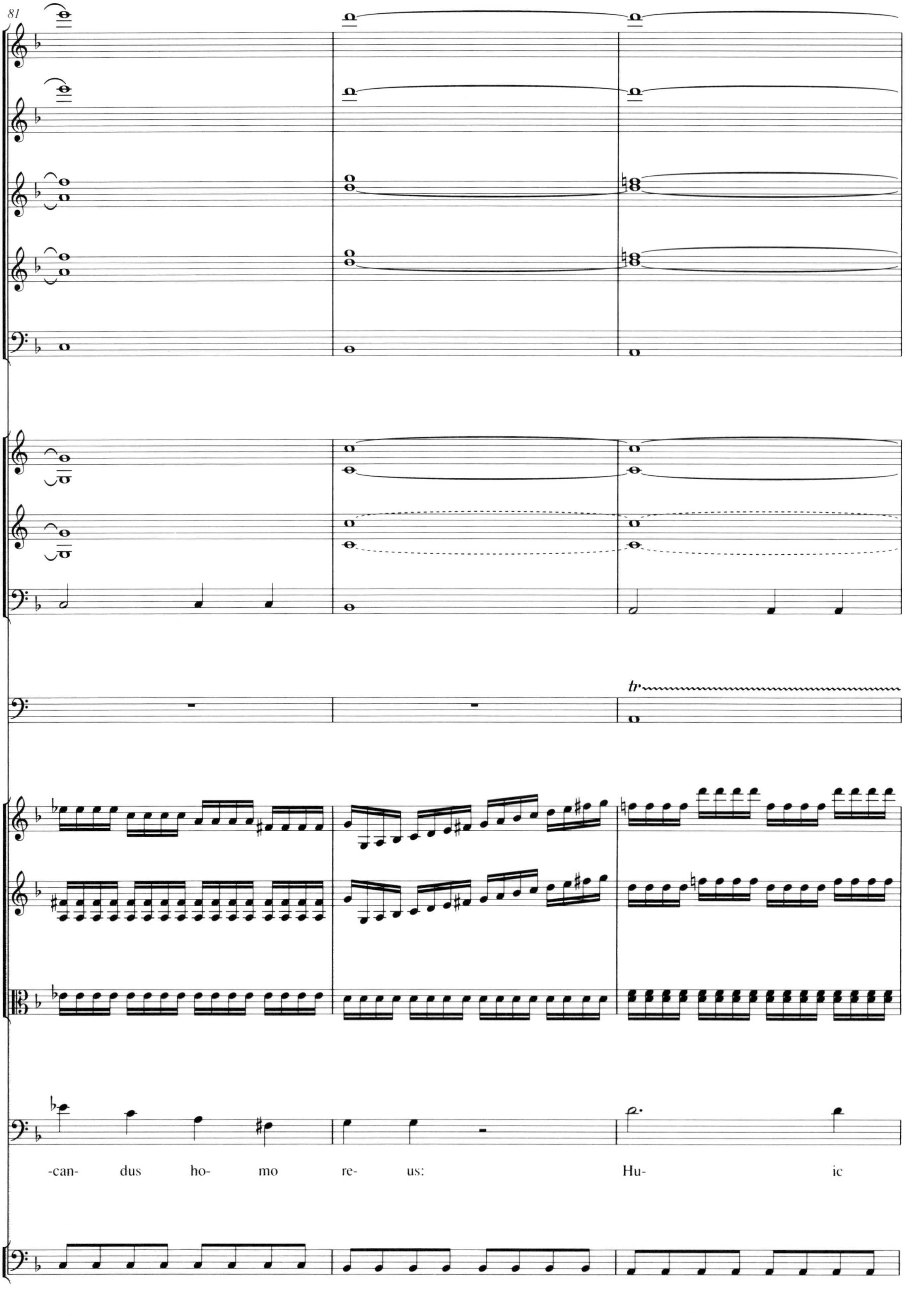
81
tr
-can- dus ho- mo re- us: Hu- ic

er- go par- ce De- us.

Andante
Vn. 1
Vn. 2
Va.
B
Vc.
Cb.
p
Pi- e Je- su Do- mi- ne, Pi- e Je- su Do- mi- ne,
Do- na, do- na e- is re- qui- em,
solo
mf
Do- na, do- na e- is re- qui- em.

9. Finale

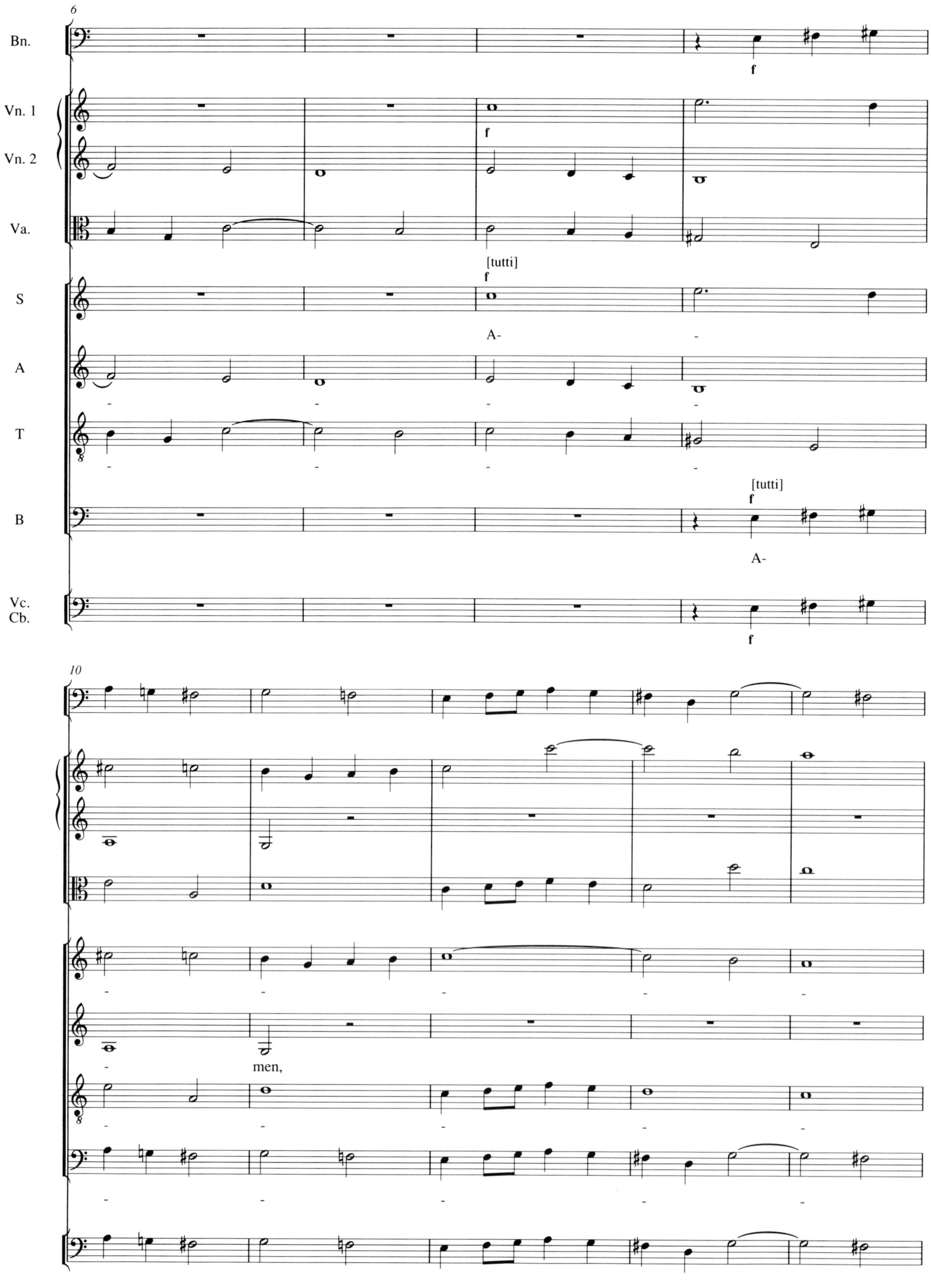
6
Bn.
Vn. 1
Vn. 2
Va.
S
A
T
B
Vc.
Cb.
f
[tutti]
A-
f
[tutti]
A-
10
men,

15
f
Ob. 1, 2
f
f
Cl. 1, 2
f
Bn.
Vn. 1
Vn. 2
Va.
S
-men, a- - - men,
A
a- - - - - -
T
-men, a- - - -
B
- - men, a-
Vc.
Vc.
Cb.
Cb.

162

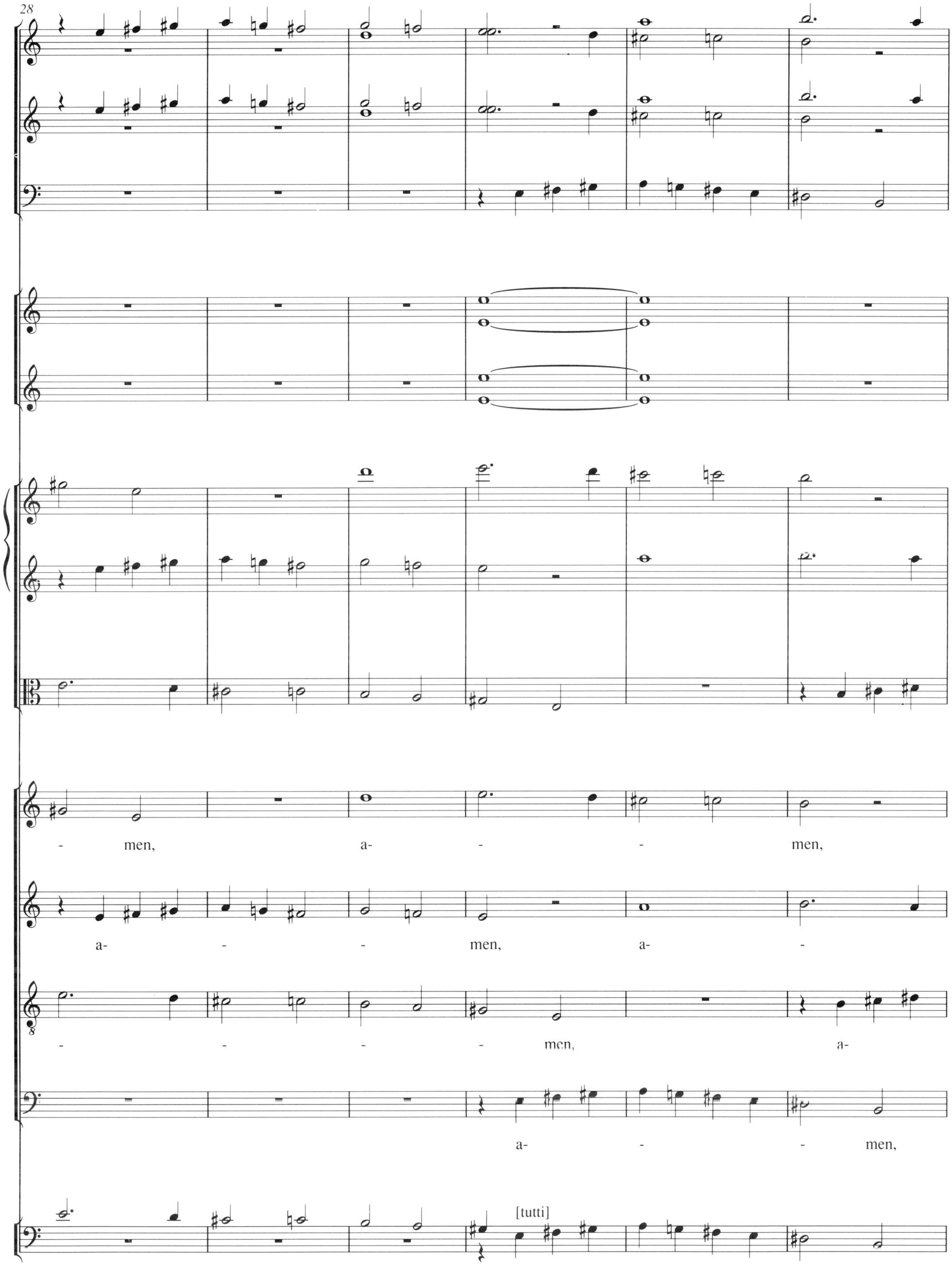
28
- men,
a-
-
-
men,
a-
-
-
men,
a-
-
-
-
-
men,
a-
a-
-
-
men,
[tutti]

164

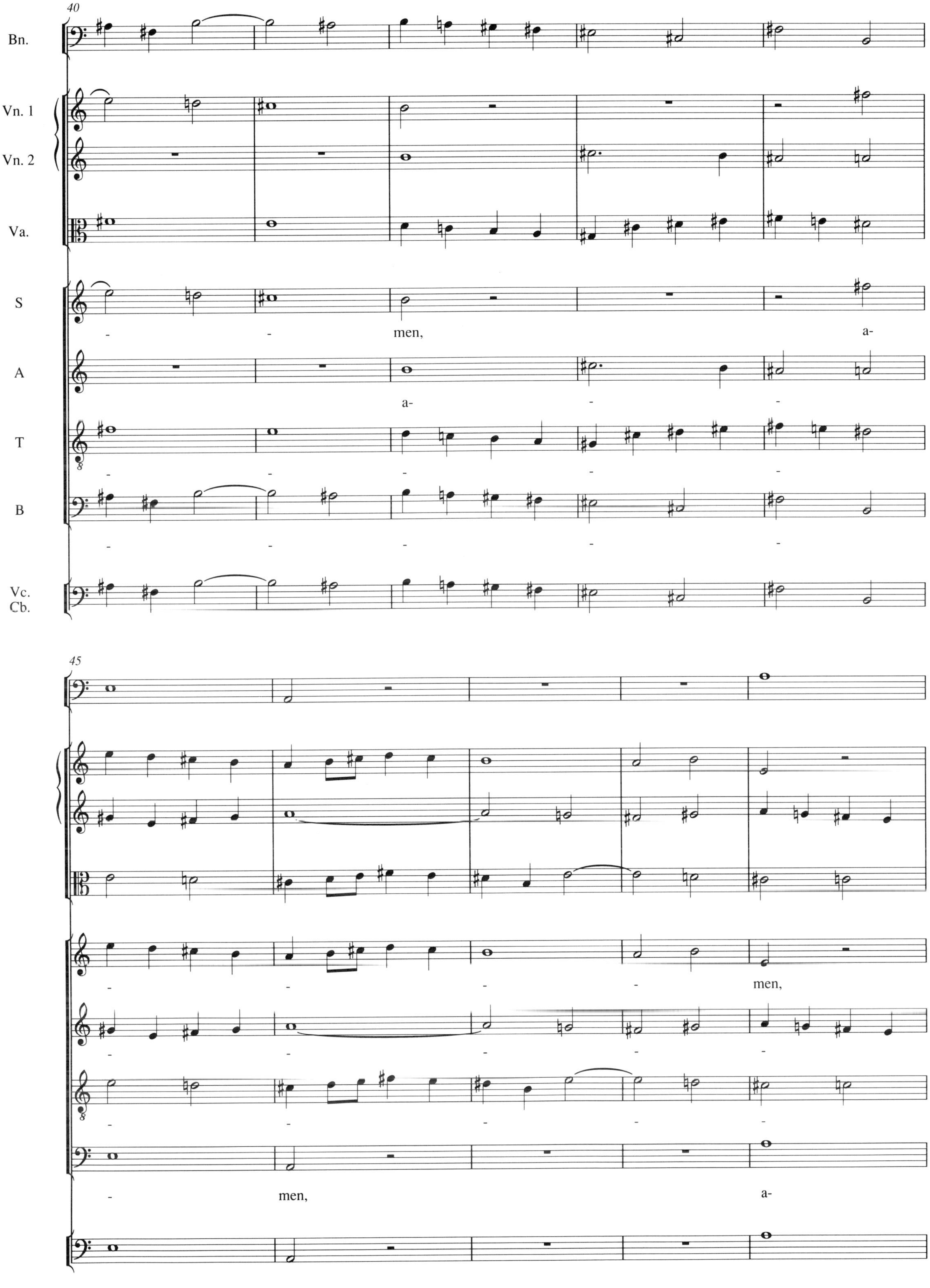
40
Bn.
Vn. 1
Vn. 2
Va.
S
- - men, a-
A
a- - -
T
- - - - -
B
- - - - -
Vc.
Cb.
45
- - - - men,
- - - - -
- - - - -
- men, a-

166

167

65
Ob. 1, 2
Cl. 1, 2
Bn.
Hn. 1, 2
Tpt. 1, 2
Vn. 1
Vn. 2
Va.
S
-men, a- - - - - - men.
A
a- - - - - - men.
T
-men, a- - - - - - men.
B
- - - - - - - men.
Vc.
Cb.

73
Allegro
Fl.
Ob. 1, 2
Cl. 1, 2
Bn.
Hn. 1, 2
Tpt. 1, 2
Trb.
Timp.
Allegro
Vn. 1
Vn. 2
Va.
S
A- men, a- men,
A
A- men, a- men,
T
A- men,
B
A- men, a- men,
Vc.
Cb.

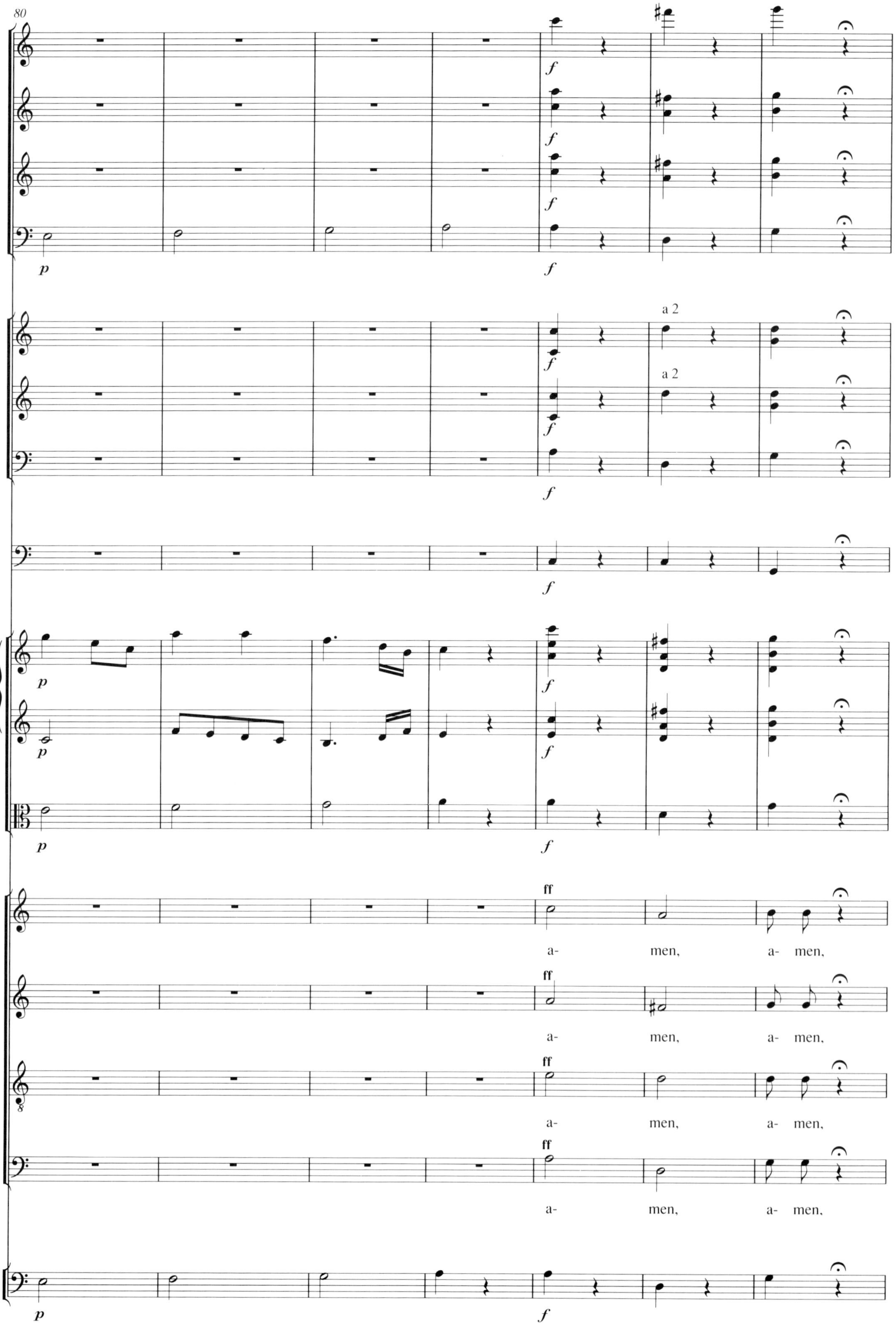
80
f
a 2
a 2
p
ff
a- men, a- men,
a- men, a- men,
a- men, a- men,
a- men, a- men,

a - - - men, a - - -

-men, a- - -

men, a- men, a- men, a-

105
a 2
a 2
a 2
a 2
-men, a- men, a- men,
-men, a- men, a- men,
-men, a- men, a- men,
-men, a- men, a- men,

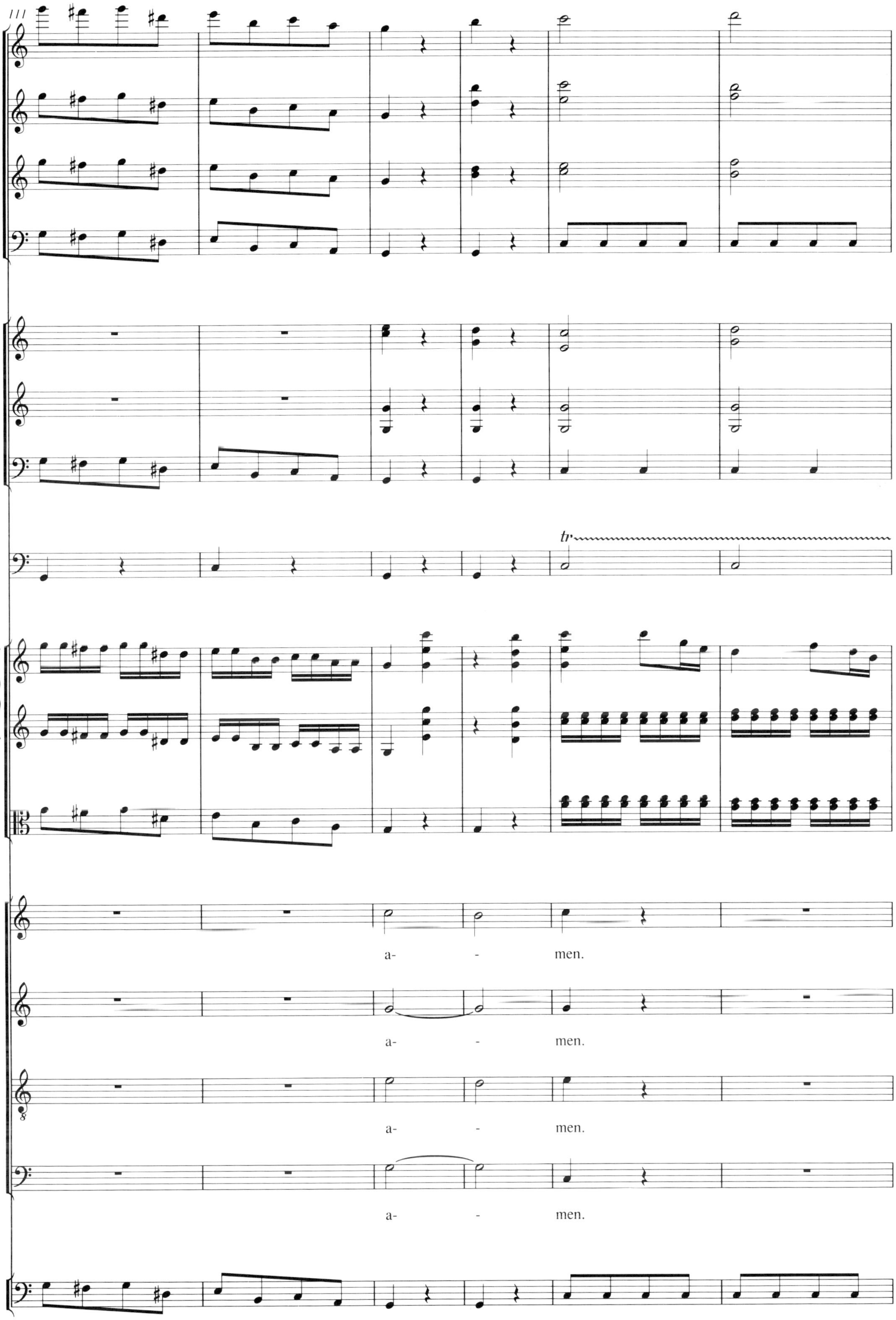
111
tr
a- - men.
a- - men.
a- - men.
a- - men.

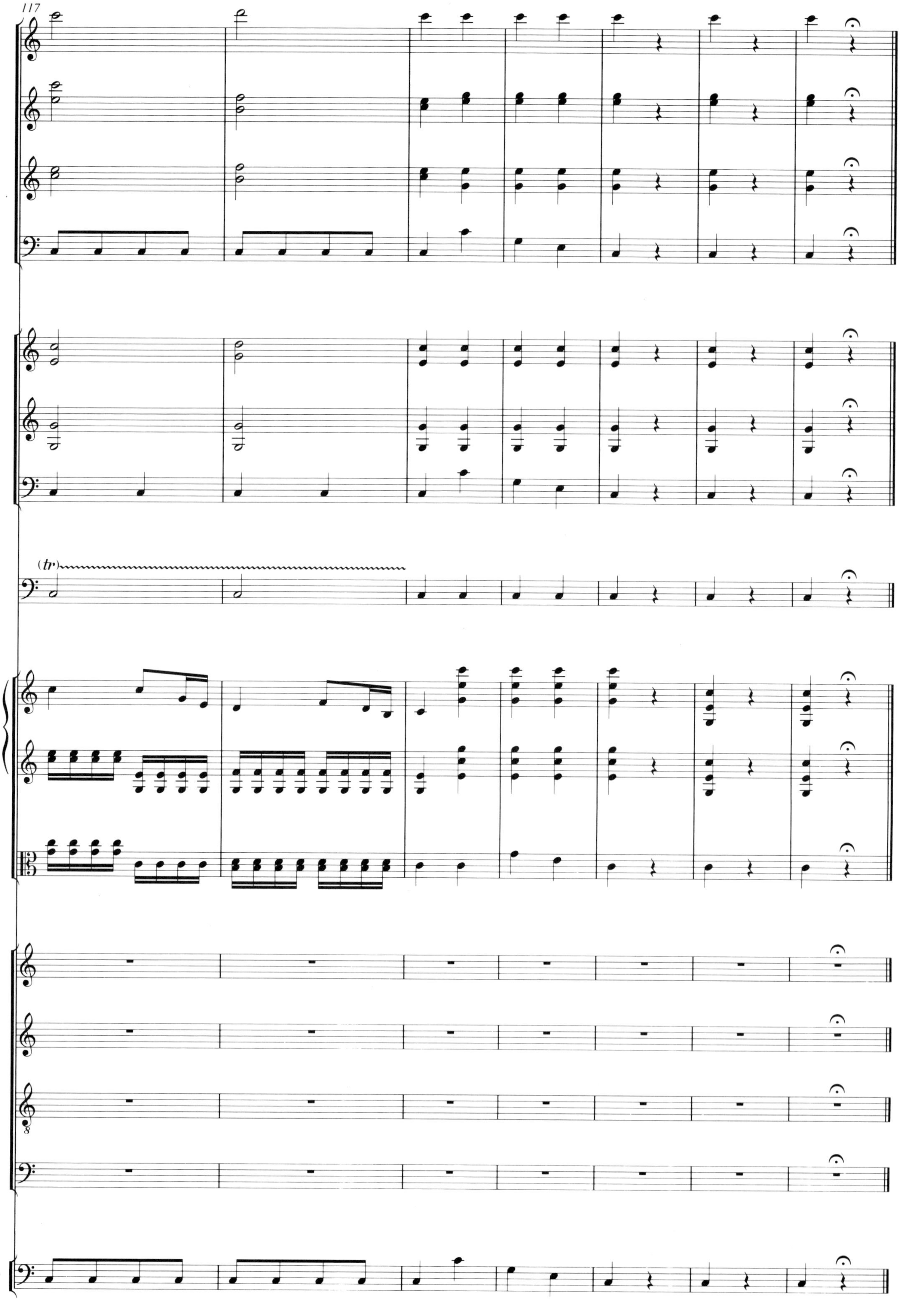
117
(tr)
8

Critical Report

The Sources

The Biblioteca Comunale in Crema possesses the autograph full score and manuscript parts, instrumental and vocal, of the *Dies irae concertato*. I have used the score as my principal guide in preparing this edition. The parts have been drawn upon as necessary to clarify readings that are unclear in the score or to supply music not written out in the score. The full score is hastily prepared, with much recourse to abbreviations such as indicating doublings at the octave by an "8" or at the third by a "3" under the upper part, and by the symbol ♪ to indicate four repeated eighth notes on the same pitch. When dynamic marks are present, one dynamic often suffices for the entire score, but the indications are usually (not always) transferred to the parts. The "default" dynamic, in both score and parts, is *forte*.

Most of the orchestral parts are by a contemporaneous copyist referred to hereafter as Copyist A, as evinced on the title pages by the inscription "Del Sig[nor]e M[aestr]o Pavesi." He prepared the parts for the flute, oboe 1, clarinet 1 and 2, bassoon, horn 1 and 2, trumpet 2, trombone, violin 1 and 2, viola, violoncello, and contrabass. He appears to have prepared the part for oboe 2 as well, but only the music for the "Confutatis" survives, mislabelled as "oboe pmo."; the first oboe's music for this number is missing. Identical handwriting and the use of the courtesy title for the composer also appear in the vocal parts marked "alto di concerto," "basso di concerto," and "basso di ripieno."

Three different sets of handwriting account for all the remaining parts except that of the timpani. Copyist B was responsible for the "soprano di ripieno," "alto di ripieno," and "tenor[e] di ripieno" parts. Copyist C can be credited with the "soprano solo" (of "Quid sum miser"), the "alto solo" (of "Inter oves"), and the "tenore solo" (of "Juste judex"). Copyist D (there are parts in the Crema library in this hand dated as late as 1913) wrote the piccolo, "soprano di concerto," and "tenore di concerto" parts, the latter two of which contain the solo soprano-tenor duet ("Recordare Jesu pie") in "Rex tremendae." The parts for oboe 2 (except for the music of the "Confutatis") and trumpet 1 are missing. The consistent use of soprano, alto, and tenor clefs in the vocal parts supports the assumption that they were all prepared in the nineteenth century.

The timpani part is in a completely different handwriting and was probably added for a later performance, maybe as late as the commemoration of the composer's centennial in 1879. Though timpani are not specified in the score, I have included them anyway since in previous performances a timpanist may have improvised from a bass instrument part. The separate piccolo ("ottavino primo") part by Copyist D has been used for the opening number and for the "Lacrimosa" section of the "Oro supplex" because in those two places Pavesi did specify the instrument in the score. The rest of the part gratuitously doubles the flute in the choral numbers and has not been included in this edition.

The parts prepared by Copyist C for the soprano, alto, and tenor soloists are each distinguished by a vocal part plus an unfigured bass and were probably extracted so that the soloists could learn their parts privately apart from rehearsals. The bass soloist, on the other hand, relied on the "basso di concerto" part for his aria ("Oro supplex"), though it too has an unfigured bass line.

The cadenzas written into the solo parts were quite probably added after Pavesi's death for soloists unfamiliar with techniques of improvising ornaments (see my article, "An Ornamented Opera Aria of *c*.1815," *Early Music* 15 [1987]: 71–73, for ornaments and cadenzas in one of Pavesi's operatic arias). The three cadenzas for "Quid sum miser" are quite elaborate and detailed (see the appendix). The second cadenza was presumably added last; it is not labelled, whereas the first is labelled "CADENZA I" and the third is labelled "CADENZA II." There are alternative cadenzas for "Inter oves" (also in the appendix). However, for "Juste judex," the aria that would seem to require the most extensive cadenza, there is only a rejected cadenza scratched out in ink. Cadenzas for the soloists in the "Recordare" of "Rex tremendae" are similarly scratched out. In neither case did I feel impelled to try to restore them; the performers would do best to write their own cadenzas to suit their voices. Finally, in the case of "Oro supplex," no cadenza could be located, although an elaboration on the notes leading into the cadence of measures 56–57 is written into the part (and has been included in the edition as an alternative reading).

Editorial Methods

The source score has violins at the top, in general followed by flute, oboes, clarinets, horns, trumpets, bassoon, violas, voices, and bass instruments (usually including the trombone if present). In the edition, the instruments and voices are placed in modern score order. The Italian names of instruments and voices are translated into English. Indications of the pitches required of the timpani are added at the start of each number. Tempo and other written directives meant to apply to the entire score are placed above the top stave and above the first violin stave. Measure numbers are added at the beginnings of all systems. Editorially added elements are placed in brackets, except that added slurs and ties are dashed, and added dynamics are set in bold (rather than the customary bold-italic) type.

The rhythmic groupings of notes and rests, beaming patterns, and stem directions are regularized according to modern conventions. The notation of slurs and ties also follows modern practices. Slurs in the vocal parts meant to clarify melismatic text underlay are tacitly removed. Measured tremolo is realized, as are other shorthand methods of notation. Groupette numerals are added without comment as necessary; two or three such numerals are considered sufficient to set up a pattern. The placing of ornaments and articulation is regularized.

With respect to paired instruments sharing a single stave, common stemming is employed except where different note values and rest patterns between the two instruments make opposing stems necessary. Voicing numerals and "a 2" designations are added as needed; these express what is already expressed in the source score and parts by other means and are therefore not considered editorial. The violoncello and contrabass parts follow the source score in having separate staves in the first number but being combined on a single stave in the other numbers.

In general, appoggiaturas of the source score and parts are notated at half the value of the following notes. This practice is followed in the edition, except that sixteenth-note appoggiaturas are notated as grace notes. In numbers 6 and 8, the solo parts have added appoggiaturas not found in the score; these are removed for the edition but are reported in the critical notes. Slurs are added to all grace notes and appoggiaturas.

Dynamics are replicated without comment for all instruments and voices wherever the score indicates an overall dynamic change. However, dynamics found in the instrumental parts are only replicated as necessary among other instruments and are not applied tacitly to voices; dynamics found in the vocal parts are likewise replicated among other voices but are not applied tacitly to instruments. Among the voices, "solo" and "tutti" indications are also replicated as necessary.

Accidentals of the source that are considered redundant by modern standards are tacitly removed. Accidentals clearly called for by context (as on repeated notes after barlines and on notes repeating a pitch at the octave within a measure) are added without comment. Other editorial accidentals are placed in brackets. Editorial cautionary accidentals are placed in parentheses. Source cautionaries (not in parentheses) are retained where they clarify readings.

The text of the score and parts corresponds for the most part with that of the *Liber Usualis*. Instances in which the text of the score and parts consistently departs from and has been altered to match the text of the *LU* are reported in the critical notes. However, instances in which variations in spellings of words occur between parts or between parts and score are not reported so long as the spelling of the *LU* is represented among them. The vocal parts, especially for the solo arias, were my chief guide for text underlaying. Isolated mistakes in the text underlaying of specific parts or the score are not reported. Syllabification of words follows modern practice. Commas are added as called for by repeated phrases.

Critical Notes

The voices and instruments are abbreviated as follows: S = Soprano; A = Alto; T = Tenor; B = Bass; Picc. = Piccolo; Fl. = Flute; Ob. = Oboe; Cl. = Clarinet; Bn. = Bassoon; Hn. = Horn; Tpt. = Trumpet; Trb. = Trombone; Timp. = Timpani; Vn. = Violin; Va. = Viola; Vc. = Violoncello; Cb. = Contrabass. Notes (including grace notes and appoggiaturas) are numbered consecutively within a measure; notes of chords are numbered from bottom to top. Pitches are designated according to the system in which middle C = c'.

Most of the reports are of significant departures of the parts from the autograph score. Reports based only on the parts or only on the score are identified as such. Reports not identified as being based on the parts or the score are based on both.

Throughout the work, there are numerous instances where eighth notes with eighth rests in the score are notated as quarter notes with or without staccatos in the parts. This is especially the case in numbers 2, 3, 5, and 6. In all such cases, the readings of the parts are made to conform with those of the score without comment. The parts also often depart from the score with respect to the values of the final notes of sections or of numbers; again, the readings of the score are provided without comment.

1. Dies irae

No key signature appears for a number obviously in D minor, a relic of earlier theory where in minor keys one fewer flat than is found today was used. M. 1, Vn. 1 (part), slurs on notes 1–2 and 3–4 set up a pattern; however, slurs over eight notes are added to conform to best violin articulation. Mm. 7–8 and 15–16, Vc. (score), whole rests only. M. 29, Vc. (part), notes 1 and 2 are half notes. Mm. 36–43, Cb. (part), low As are added below the Ds. Mm. 45–46 and 48–49, Vc. (part), eighth notes are indicated. M. 57, Fl., indication of "Flute" is from score; indication of "solo" is from part. Mm. 59–60, SAT, and mm. 64–65, ATB, text is "sibilla." M. 81, Cb. (part), note 1 is a. M. 84, Timp. (part), measure is missing. M. 85, Timp. (part), note is d. Mm. 86–87, Vn. 1 (part), slur on notes 1–2. M. 88, Vc. (part), note 1 is b. Mm. 90–102, Vc. (part), eighth notes on d are indicated throughout. Mm. 95–96 and 101–2, Vc., score is left empty but measures have been made to match the parallel mm. 36–37 and 42–43; *col basso* indication is not until m. 103. M. 118, Trb. (part), note 2 is e. M. 126, Trb. (part), notes 1 and 2 are half notes with no quarter rests.

2. Tuba mirum

Mm. 1–3, all woodwinds and strings, prefix notes written after barline as grace notes to main quarter note; in edition, notated as triplets before barline to permit uniform articulation. M. 8, Vn. 2 (part), chord 5 and note 15 are eighth notes with eighth rests. Mm. 8–10, 13–15, 76–78, 81–83, A, *ossia* notes only in parts. Mm. 13, 14, 76, 77, 81, 82, Va. (part), notes 1, 2, 4, and 5, each are two sixteenth notes. M. 23, Cl. 1 (part), note is half note with no quarter rest. M. 35, Hn. 1 and 2 have *p*. M. 132, Bn., Vc., Cb. (parts), note 4 is b.

3. Quid sum miser

M. 12, Hn. 1 (part), note is dotted half note. Mm. 37–38, Fl. and Ob. 1 (parts), slur on notes 1–2. Mm. 43–44, Ob. 1 and Cl. 2 (parts), slur on notes 1–2. M. 59, Bn. (part) has *f*. M. 72, Hn. 1 and Hn. 2 (parts), note is half note with quarter rest. Mm. 80–81, Fl. and Cl. 2 (parts), slur on notes 1–2. M. 86, Fl. and Vn. 1 (parts), slur on notes 1–2. Mm. 86–87, Ob. 1 and Cl. 2 (parts), slur on notes 1–2. M. 88, Hn. 2 (part), note is half note with quarter rest. M. 89, Vn. 1 (part), slur on notes 2–3.

4. Rex tremendae

M. 2, Va., note 2 has accent. M. 2, Cb. (part), note 3 has accent. M. 8, Bn. (part), second half of bar is notated as unmeasured tremolo. M. 8, Vc. and Cb. (parts), note 1 has *p*. Mm. 9–11, Vn. 1, Vn. 2, and Va. (parts), first half of each bar is notated as unmeasured tremolo. Mm. 13 and 15, Timp. (part), both B♭s are notated an octave higher (at b♭). M. 21, Va. (part), note 6 is b♭. M. 102, Fl. (part), note 1 is d‴. M. 102, Ob. 1 (part), note 1 is b♭″. M. 102, Va. (part), chords 1–4 are b♭ + d′. M. 103, Va. (part) has two b♭ quarter notes. M. 103, Vc. and Cb. (parts), notes 1–2 are B♭–B♭. M. 104, Va. (part) has four chords in rhythm of other strings, g + b♭. M. 110, Trb. and vn. 1 (parts) have *p*.

5. Juste judex

M. 1, Fl., Ob. 1, Bn., Hn. 1, Hn. 2, Tpt. 2, Trb., Vn. 2, Va. (parts), notes are half notes followed by half rests with fermatas. M. 1, Cl. 1 (part), note 1 is half note followed by half rest with fermata. M. 1, Cl. 2 (part), note 1 is half note followed by quarter rest with fermata. M. 1, Vn. 1 (part), fermata is on rest. M. 6, Cl. 1 (part), notes 9 and 10 are eighth notes with staccatos. M. 39, Fl., Ob. 1 and 2, Cl. 1 and 2, Hn. 1 and 2 have *p*. Mm. 39–41, Fl. (part), all notes on offbeats. M. 45, Cl. 2 (part), note is eighth note. Mm. 67, 74, 123, Hn. 2 (part), note is g′. M. 75, Va., Vc., Cb., whole rest only. M. 82, T, text is "digne." Mm. 87–88, 134–35, 138–39, 148–49, 152–53, 155–56, 157–58, T, text is "perenne." M. 90, Hn. 1 and Hn. 2 (parts) have *p*. Mm. 114, 116, 121, 123, Fl., note is half note with half rest. Mm. 115–16, Hn. 2 (score), not indicated as playing. M. 116, Hn. 1 and Hn. 2 (parts), note is half note with half rest. M. 116, Hn. 2 (part), note is g′. M. 134, Hn. 1 and 2 have *p*. M. 148, Hn. 1 (part) has *p*. Mm. 159–60, Ob. 1 and Cl. 2 (parts), notes are tied. M. 163, Vc. and Cb. (score), note 1 has *f*.

6. Inter oves

M. 7, Vc. and Cb. (parts) have *p*. M. 22, Vn. 1 (part), chord is f′ + c″ + f″. M. 22, Vn. 2 (part), chord is c′ + a′. Mm. 42 and 90–91, A, *ossia* notes only in part. Mm. 45, 50, 52, 71, 76, 78, 82, 84, A (part), note 1 has appoggiatura. M. 50, Cl. 1 and 2 have *p*. Mm. 50 and 52, A (score), note 1 lacks appoggiatura. M. 75, Ob. 1 and 2, Hn. 1, Vn. 2 (score) have *p*. M. 75, Ob. 1, Cl. 1, Cl. 2, Hn. 1, Hn. 2 (parts) have *p*. M. 98, all instruments and voice (score), no fermatas. M. 98, A (score), notes are f′ (dotted quarter), g′ (eighth), g′ (dotted quarter with trill), g′ (eighth); text underlay has the middle two syllables of "se-ques-te-ra" falling on notes 1 and 4, respectively.

7. Confutatis

The designations "Allegro" (m. 1) and "Maggiore" (m. 51, spelled "Magior" and "Magiore") are found in the parts (not in the score). Mm. 4–7, 16–17, 19–20, 22, 25–27, 40, 42–45, 47–50, Timp. (part), all Gs are notated an octave higher (at g). M. 13, Bn. (part), note 1 is g. M. 16, Va. (part), chord is g + d′ + b♮′. M. 17, score and parts (all strings, Fl., Ob. 2, Timp.) have *f*. M. 18, Timp. (part), notes 1–4 are g. M. 19, Bn. (part), whole rest only. Mm. 23–24, A, *ossia* notes only in "alto di concerto" part. Mm. 33 and 37, Vn. 2 (part), whole rest only. Mm. 36–37, Hn. 2 (part), note is e′. M. 56, Hn. 1 and 2 (score), Hn. 1 (part), note is d″. Mm. 59 and 67, Vn. 2 (part) has *p*. M. 61, Vn. 1 (part) has *p*. M. 63, Fl. (part) has *p*.

8. Oro supplex

Mm. 8, 9, 36, 37, "soli" indications for clarinets and horns in parts only. M. 17, Hn. 1 and Hn. 2 (parts) have "soli" indications. M. 17, Vn. 2 (part), note 1 is c′. Mm. 23–24, Vn. 2 (part), lower notes of chords are lacking. M. 29, Vn. 1 (part), chord (notes 4–5) in eighth notes with eighth rest. M. 40, Hn. 1 and 2 (score), note 3 is eighth note with eighth rest. Mm. 48 and 91, B (part), note 1 has appoggiatura. M. 56, B (part), note 2 has appoggiatura. M. 56, B, *ossia* notes only in part. M. 63, Vn. 1 (part), chords 1 and 3 are g' + b♭'; all four chords are on the off-beat. Mm. 68–87, Fl., change to piccolo is indicated in score but not in flute part; I suggest that both piccolo and flute be used in these measures. M. 70, Picc. (part) has *ff*. M. 78, B (part), note 2 is e', ♯ on note 3; B (score), note 2 (c') lacks ♯. Mm. 83, 85–87, Timp. (part), all As are notated an octave higher (at a). M. 88, the designation "Andante" was added in a later hand in the score; it also appears in the Vc. and Cb. parts, while the parts for Vn. 1, Vn. 2, and Va. have "A°," "pmo tempo," and "Largo," respectively.

9. Finale

The title "Finale" is in the score; the number is titled "Amen" in the parts. M. 12, B (both parts), note 2 has ♯. Mm. 58–59, Cl. 2 (part), whole note in m. 58 is tied to quarter note at start of m. 59. M. 69, T (both parts), note 2 is b. Mm. 71–72, Cl. 2 (part), m. 71 has whole-note c", m. 72 has whole note d". M. 78, Vn. 2 (part), chord is a' + f". Mm. 79, 86, 91–93, 99–100, 104, 108, 111, 113–14, Timp. (part), all Gs are notated an octave higher (at g). M. 84, Vn. 1 (part), chord is a' + c" + c'". M. 87, T ("tenore di concerto" part) has *ff*. Mm. 87–89, 91–93, Vn. 1, Vn. 2, Cl. 2 (parts), notes 2–4 are triplet eighth notes. Mm. 91–93, Cl. 1 (part), notes 2–4 are triplet eighth notes. M. 105, S ("soprano di ripieno" part), note has ♮. Mm. 115–18, Vn. 1 (part), notes 2–4 are triplet eighth notes.

Appendix
Cadenzas

Cadenzas for "Quid sum miser"

[Cadenza 1 at m. 60]

[Cadenza 2 at m. 78]

Cum vix jus- tus sit se- cu- rus.

[Cadenza 3 at m. 106]

Alternative Cadenzas for "Inter oves" at measure 98

[a]

-ques- - tra.

[b]

-ques- tra.

[c]

[-ques- tra.]

[d]

se- ques- tra, se- ques- tra, me ⎯⎯ se- ques- tra.

[e]

-ques- tra.

Recent Researches in the Music of the Nineteenth and
Early Twentieth Centuries
Rufus Hallmark, general editor

Vol.	Composer: Title
1–2	Jan Ladislav Dussek: *Selected Piano Works*
3–4	Johann Nepomuk Hummel: *Piano Concerto, Opus 113*
5	*One Hundred Years of Eichendorff Songs*
6	Etienne-Nicolas Méhul: *Symphony No. 1 in G Minor*
7–8	*Embellished Opera Arias*
9	*The Nineteenth-Century Piano Ballade: An Anthology*
10	*Famous Poets, Neglected Composers: Songs to Lyrics by Goethe, Heine, Mörike, and Others*
11	Charles-Marie Widor: *Symphonie I in C Minor*
12	Charles-Marie Widor: *Symphonie II in D Major*
13	Charles-Marie Widor: *Symphonie III in E Minor*
14	Charles-Marie Widor: *Symphonie IV in F Minor*
15	Charles-Marie Widor: *Symphonie V in F Minor*
16	Charles-Marie Widor: *Symphonie VI in G Minor*
17	Charles-Marie Widor: *Symphonie VII in A Minor*
18	Charles-Marie Widor: *Symphonie VIII in B Major*
19	Charles-Marie Widor: *Symphonie Gothique*
20	Charles-Marie Widor: *Symphonie Romane*
21	Archduke Rudolph of Austria: *Forty Variations on a Theme by Beethoven for Piano; Sonata in F Minor for Violin and Piano*
22	Fanny Hensel: *Songs for Pianoforte, 1836–1837*
23	*Anthology of Goethe Songs*
24	Walter Rabl: *Complete Instrumental Chamber Works*
25	Stefano Pavesi: *Dies irae concertato*